HOW TO MAKE MONEY
WITH
STOCK OPTIONS

a Basic Guide for the Conservative Investor

MERVYN L. HECHT

INVINOVERITAS PRESS
SANTA MONICA, CALIFORNIA

THIRD EDITION

Published by Invinoveritas Press
Santa Monica, California

Printed in Hong Kong
ISBN: 0-9662481-2-0

Library of Congress Catalog Card No: 91-91497

0 9 8 7 6 5 4 3 2 1

*Dedicated to Naim, Keith and the Colonel,
who helped me learn; and with thanks to
my friends Sybil Fields, Ray Swartz, and
my wife Dr. Bonnie Hecht who helped
me write what I learned into English.
Also with thanks to Dr. Russell Taussig,
who contributed both text and ideas
to this edition, Jean Ross who helped
with editing, and Lloyd Evans and Walter
Baer who gave valuable suggestions.*

With the purchase of this book you are entitled to one copy of our tracking software beta testing copy. This will help you to keep track of your option trades, and will alert you to certain events. To download this software, please go to: <howtomakemoneywithstockoptions.com> and follow the instructions there. If you are unable to download the software, please write to: Mervyn Hecht, 311 Amalfi Dr. Santa Monica, CA 90402 and a disk will be sent to you.

CONTENTS

List of Figures

HOW TO MAKE MONEY
WITH
STOCK OPTIONS

Preface to the 2005 Third Edition
With Tracking Software Included

This is the third edition of this book. The fact that several thousand copies have been sold testifies to the interest in options in the personal investment community. The Second Edition was written in 1998. Since that time options have indeed become of more interest in the investment community, and to a small extent, more familiar to the personal investor. A large part of this is a result of the internet, and easy access to option information. And websites such as Charles Schwab have excellent tracking, evaluation, and profit computation software for their option clients to use. Personally I like to keep my information on my own computer, so I developed option tracking software which I am sharing with buyers of this book.

An article in the Wall Street Journal Online magazine of November 3, 2004 points out that "some of the nation's biggest private banks are pitching options and other exotic investments to their wealthiest clients as a way to boost returns." Nevertheless, option writing is still an esoteric activity, and it's still hard to find simple, straightforward information about the nuts and bolts of it.

The following paragraphs from the prefaces of the two earlier editions on this subject continue to be of interest to investors today:

It has always been clear to me that option writing can be done on a very conservative basis, with limited and defined risks that can be adequately understood by the individual investor, and communicated by a broker to a client. Friends that have asked me about option writing, and heard me make that statement, are usually intrigued by it and want to understand it better. Unfortunately, cocktail parties where these conversations often take place are usually too short for an adequate explanation of option writing. So, at the request of several friends, I began to look around for a book which I could recommend to them to explain what kind of strategies I was engaged in, and what conservative strategies they could follow.I was disappointed in my search.

I found lots of interesting books on how to make money in buying real estate, how to make money in selling real estate, how to make money in buying options on real estate, without really buying it, and how to make money in selling options on real estate and not really selling it. I found books on How To Make Money by investing in stamps and gold coins, and a number of other things, including macadamia nuts and iguanas. But I did not find any books that explained, in simple language, how to make money in stock options. I did find a few very excellent books that explained stock options and stock option strategies. The disclosure brochure put out by the Chicago Board of Options Exchange itself, which is sent to all investors in options through the Exchange, is pretty good. There are some much more detailed and voluminous works which cover virtually every element of option writing, and which can serve as excellent resource books. Lately, some books have become available which cover very sophisticated strategies for using computers to help devise option strategies and plays which I find very exciting. But all of these books are too long, too detailed, and too voluminous for me to give to my friends. My friend Jeff, the dermatologist, claims that he is not willing to devote more than three hours to reading anything about any investment. If it takes more time than that, he claims, the nature of the investment is too complex for a medical doctor.

I think he is right. I don't think an investor has to understand all of the complexities and intricacies of the options market in order to include options trading as a part of his or her normal investment strategies. Average investors in the stock market can master two or three conservative, fixed risk option strategies and use them comfortably in their investment programs.

And so I wrote this book (mainly to protect myself at cocktail parties). My hope is that I have written it in simple enough language so that the average investor in the stock market, with a medium sized portfolio, can understand some of what I have said. It is not necessary to understand everything I have said. It is only necessary that in reading through the book, one or two strategies are understood, The investor can then try these strategies once or twice, and with the help of a stockbroker with adequate training, engage in those strategies which are appropriate and of interest.

The reader must accept the fact that some of the ideas are in fact complex and require reflection and experience to fully understand. But that is true of the stock market itself. An investor who just buys stock without understanding the fundamentals of the company and the economy is risking whatever he pays for the stock.

To understand all of the fundamentals of the company and the economy is a potentially infinite task to which many brilliant people devote their lives. Of course, no investor expects to fully understand the fundamentals of the company, and certainly not of our economy, which are constantly changing. We are satisfied with looking at certain financial information about the company, and various indicators about the economy. Fortunately, the option strategies discussed in this book are not as complicated as the overall financial data of a large company, nor are they as complicated as an understanding of the principles of economics. The principles of option writing can be on the reader's level of sophistication and experience in investments.

Because I believe that these principles can be understood by an investor of moderate sophistication, I was willing to undertake the effort to write this book.

While option strategies are not for everyone, I believe that most investors can master the basic concepts, and use them to advantage. *Above all I believe that an investor who understands and uses options can invest with less risk than one who doesn't use options.* And that is the fundamental reason for this book.

Pacific Palisades, California, January 2005

PART I - Introduction

Current Attitudes Toward Stock Options

Stock options have a bad name. Many investors refuse to have anything to do with them, having heard that they are "speculative." For example, in some lawsuits judges and jurors take it for granted that if a stockbroker or investment advisor engaged in stock option transactions for an investor, it was automatically a "speculative" investment.

In the following pages I hope to convince you that many stock option strategies are not speculative, and are less risky than the traditional purchase and sale of stocks. The one difference is that stock option strategies are more difficult to understand, and it takes more time to learn the vocabulary. For this reason, part of this book deals with understanding the vocabulary of stock options.

But this is not really a book about options. It is a book about risks in the options market. There are already a number of books that explain options, generally in much more detail than options are explained in this book. The Chicago Board Options Exchange (CBOE) pamphlet on options, which is routinely sent to investors who trade in options, contains a lot of valuable information on options and examples of various option strategies.

There are now several mutual funds that advertise that they buy and sell options to achieve a higher yield for their investors - and for some investors, letting the experts handle these kinds of trades is the best decision. As a result of this literature, lots of people know and understand the basic principles of options.

Yet, in the 30+ years that I have been involved in option trading, I have been amazed at the lack of general understanding of what a "risky" strategy is, and what is not, and what is "speculative" and what is not. Many people - some of whom surely should know better - think that any option trade is inherently speculative. At the other extreme, I have known experienced brokers using risky strategies they sincerely believed (and told customers) could not lose money!

The truth lies somewhere in between. Some strategies are high risk, and some are low risk. Some are speculative and some are conservative. Some are appropriate for the particular investor, and many are inappropriate.

The purpose of this book is to try to define these terms,

and to identify some of the more common strategies that fall into each group.

As a consequence, this book is not thorough in its discussions of the principles of options. It is written primarily for people who either know a little something about options, or a lot about stocks.

Part one summarizes option history, principles and risks. Part two is a compilation and discussion of basic option strategies. Parts three through five describe some of the more common complex option strategies, including those that should be classified as "conservative." Parts VI and VII concern tax considerations and practical applications and common sense for lawyers and brokers.   In each part I try to identify what the risk is, and why.

In this way, I hope to play a small part in clearing up the widespread misunderstanding of the relationship between risk and option trading.

A. The Differences between Options and Stocks

Owning a stock is not the same as owning a house. When you own a house you can live in it, you can fix it up, and you can see it every day. Many people think that the same is true when they hold a stock certificate in their hand. They can see it and feel it, it has an attractive gold or green border, and it is made of fine quality paper. (See Figure I-1.)

Figure I-1 Stock and Option Certificates.

a stock certificate

[does not exist]

an option certificate

But the fact is that the stock certificate itself is merely representative of a group of intangible rights that the holder may or may not be entitled to exercise. If your name appears in the right place on the stock certificate, and also appears in the right place in the company records, and if the company has managed to stay out of any kind of bankruptcy proceeding, and if certain other facts have remained constant, then you may have the right to vote at a shareholders meeting, the right to exchange voting rights under certain situations, the right to receive dividends, and the right to sell your rights represented by the certificate.

Some or all of these rights can be taken away from you by action of the board of directors of the company, or by your creditors, or by creditors of the company. Whatever rights you have you can probably exercise whether or not you have the certificate, as long as your name is properly inscribed on the shareholder register of the company. For that reason, and for convenience, many, if not most, shareholders never take possession of stock certificates in companies in which they own stock, but allow the stock certificates to remain in "street name" with their stock broker. This means that the company lists the brokerage house as the owner, and the brokerage house lists you as the owner. These shareholders have the same rights as do shareholders that hold a certificate, but instead of certificates they have the right to instruct the stockbrokerage company to do the same things that a stockholder with a certificate can do in person.

Buying or selling a stock option gives the buyer or seller certain rights which are very much the same kind of rights as a stockholder has. As explained below, the buyer of a Call has a right to buy stock at a certain price under certain circumstances. Obviously the right to buy something at a fixed price is not the same as already owning it, but it is not very different in terms of the potential for profit.

In any event, when thinking about options it is important to realize that we are talking about the same kinds of intangible rights that the holder of a stock certificate has. Some people believe that this "trading in rights" is a new, weird "end of the century" phenomenon. But option rights in and of themselves are not so new. The first option transactions arose from transactions in ancient Egypt. By the time of tulip trading in Holland in the 1600's they were quite popular in the commercial community. For a very interesting look at option trading among the Jews in Amsterdam during the 17th Century, read the novel, THE COFFEE TRADER, by David Liss.

The kinds of options that we deal with today arose from commercial contract transactions of a type with which we are all familiar. Suppose that a vineyard owner is in the process of growing ten acres of grapes. He thinks that if he can sell the grapes for $1,000 per acre when the grapes are mature, that $10,000 in gross receipts will be adequate for him to pay all his expenses and live comfortably until the next harvest. (Not only is this story apocryphal but grapes are usually sold by volume not by acre). He also knows that while grape prices may be slightly higher than $1,000 per acre at the moment, they are subject to fluctuation depending on quality and availability at harvest time, and that he may therefore eventually get more or less than $1,000 per acre.

Meanwhile, at the wine production facility, the wine producer knows that if he can buy grapes at $1,000 per acre, he can bottle the wine, sell it at a reasonable price, and make a fair profit. He too knows that grape prices may fluctuate, so there is a possibility that he may have to pay substantially more than $1,000 per acre, and thus not make a profit for the year.

It behooves these two entrepreneurs to meet together, and agree in advance to buy and sell future production for $1,000 per acre. Note that such a "future" sale is reminiscent of the old story of the fellow that sold the Brooklyn Bridge - the farmer is selling something that he doesn't (yet) own. The wine producer acquires a right to buy something in the future which does not yet exist.

A slight modification of the contract between these two people would create an option transaction. If the owner of the vineyard sells the right to buy the grapes to the wine producer for $1,000 an acre, but the producer is not obligated to buy, the producer has acquired a Call option. It is the decoupling of the right to buy from the duty to sell that creates the option.

And so, you may ask, under what circumstances would the owner of the vineyard be willing to give the wine producer the right to buy, without requiring him to have the duty to buy. As is so often the case in life, the answer is that the vineyard owner would only do that if he were paid sufficient money to make it worth his while. Suppose, for example, that the vineyard owner is reasonably certain that the price of grapes will never fall below $900 per acre. Yet, at $900 an acre he will not make enough profit to live comfortably until the next harvest. Suppose further that the wine producer is willing to pay $100 per acre for the rights to acquire the production for a further payment of $900 per acre. Since at a total cost of $1,000 per acre he can make a reasonable profit, the producer now buys a "Call option." He pays $100 for the right to buy the production for an additional $900 per acre. The vineyard owner has "hedged," so that his risk of not having a successful year is extremely small. The producer has paid $100 per acre to create a reasonable certainty of a profitable year. Each side has protected himself from economic disaster for the year, at a small price relative to the overall transaction. If grapes are selling below $900 per acre at the end of the year the option will not be exercised, and the vineyard owner will get the current price of grapes plus the $100 per acre he received for the option. He is $100 per acre better off than he would have been. The producer still can make a nice profit, but less than if he hadn't bought the option. If the price is over $1,000 per acre the vineyard owner only gets $1,000 per acre ($900 plus the $100 option price) and the wine producer has purchased grapes at $1,000 per acre. In this case, the vineyard owner made a reasonable profit, but gave up and lost an extraordinary profit. The extraordinary profit was, in effect, passed to the producer.

Through the use of the option, both the seller and the buyer made their business transactions more conservative.

It is this ability to create protection and to collect a premium that permits options to be utilized by the conservative investor to create conservative investment strategies.

B. The Hard Part Is The Vocabulary

Because options deal with (1) the underlying security, (2) a strike price, (3) a premium, and (4) a limited time, and because they are often traded in groups (combinations) that are described with special names, the vocabulary of options becomes important. So we start there.

ALWAYS REMEMBER, HOWEVER, THAT THE OPTION IS A BUNDLE OF RIGHTS IN AND OF ITSELF - NOT AN APPENDAGE TO THE UNDERLYING STOCK. THINK OF AN OPTION AS IF IT WERE REPRESENTED BY ITS OWN "CERTIFICATE" WHICH FLUCTUATES IN PRICE LIKE STOCK CERTIFICATES DO.

C. Understanding The Terminology:
12 Key Terms

The following discussion is very basic and certainly not thorough. More complete discussions of option writing are available in many publications, including the pamphlet distributed by the Chicago Board of Options Exchange to everyone who opens an options account with a member firm. Brokers also have access to discussions in their company's procedure manuals. But the following brief summary is all one needs to understand options. It is presented in accordance with my personal views of what the important concepts of option writing are, and how they should be conceptualized. Reading definitions is no fun, but a basic understanding of the vocabulary is essential to further understanding of the concepts.

I classify options into four categories: STOCK CALLS, STOCK PUTS, INDEX CALLS, and INDEX PUTS. Some texts on options that I've seen properly define PUTS and CALLS and then assume that a Put and a Call on an index fits the same definition as a stock Put or a stock Call. Because I think that the risks and strategies involved in Puts and Calls on stocks are very different than those on indices, I recommend thinking about these four kinds of options as if they were four different pieces of paper, like stock certificates, each representing a different kind of investment.

When talking about an option, the option should be

designated by the underlying security, its termination month, its strike price, and its type. For example - one Ford Jan 35 CALL is an option to buy 100 shares of Ford Motor Co. At $35 per share until the end of the third trading Friday next January. (See Figure I-2.) With that basic information in mind, here is a brief definition of the dozen basic option terms for repeated reference:

1. CALL. One stock Call is a right to <u>buy</u> 100 shares of stock at a particular price until a specified time. We saw the Call in action with our friend the wine producer. He bought a Call to be sure he could acquire his grapes at a maximum of $1,000 per acre.

If I own one Ford January 35 Call, I have the right to buy 100 shares of Ford Motor stock at $35 per share through the close of the business day of the third Friday of the following January. Alternatively I can sell the Call itself. If I own such a Call, someone sold it to me. That person has committed to sell 100 shares of Ford stock to me if I exercise my option. If I exercise my option, the stock is said to be "called away" from the seller.

The seller of the call is obligating himself to sell the stock at the strike price. This seller might already own Ford stock and have sold a Call against it, or the seller, if called, may have to go into the open market and buy the stock to "cover" the position. If the stock has moved up significantly above the strike price, this "uncovered" seller will lose the spread between $35 and the price he has to pay to

Figure I-2 An Option listing from the Wall Street Journal

Option &	Strike	Calls-Last	Puts-Last
N.Y. Close	Price	Oct.Nov.Jan.	Oct.Nov.Jan.
XYZ			
32	35	1/8 1/4 5/8	3-1/4 r 4-1/4

This listing is one line of the options on the XYZ Motor Company. The day preceeding this listing, XYZ stock closed at $32 per share. The strike price illustrated is $35 per share. Other horizontal lines show different strike prices and relative option prices.

CALL options with a strike price of $35 for October last traded at 1/8. This means that a XYZ October 35 CALL would cost 100 times 1/8 or $12.50 plus commission. The November XYZ 35 CALL option last traded at 1/4 and the January at 5/8ths.

Note that the November PUT is not priced, it is restricted.

acquire the stock and deliver it to the holder of the call.

There is no certificate issued to represent the option. It is merely an entry on your broker's books. Only the "confirm" you receive from your broker, and your broker's credit, guarantee you the option rights.

2. PUT. One stock Put is a right to sell 100 shares of stock at a particular price until a specified time. In our wine story, this would exist if the grower paid the producer $100 per acre for the right to sell the producer the grapes produced for $1,100 per acre. The grower would thus have protected himself from a price decline below $1,000 per acre, and the producer would have collected $100 per acre in exchange for the contingent promise to purchase at a price he can afford to pay.

Similarly, if I own one Ford January 35 PUT, I have a right to sell 100 shares of Ford Motor stock at $35 per share at any time through the expiration date. The person that sold the PUT to me has become obligated to buy the stock. As with the CALL, I can also sell the PUT itself at any time during its life. (See Figure I-2.) I may already own the 100 shares, and have bought the PUT to protect its value. Alternatively, if I do not own the stock and if the stock price goes down during the option period, it will pay me to purchase the stock and then "put it" (sell the stock by implementing the PUT) to the buyer at the higher *($35)* price. The result of the transaction will be that I sold high, then bought low, which never hurts! On the other hand, if

I SOLD the put at 35, I guaranteed to buy it at that price. Thus, if the stock goes down during the option period and does not recover, if exercised (and you can bet it will be) I will have to buy the stock at 35 even if the market price is below that figure.

3. INDEX CALL The S&P 100 index is described below. For the moment it is sufficient to understand that an index CALL gives the buyer the right to collect a varying sum of money until a specific time, as the index rises above a specific number. For example, if I buy one index CALL at $300, and the index goes up to $310 before the CALL expires, I instruct my broker to exercise the CALL and my broker will put $1,000, less transaction costs, into my account. This is because one call is equal to 100 shares, the price of each share went up $10, and therefore "10 times 100 shares equals $1000. Alternatively, if the index goes to $290, nothing happens: I bought the CALL, and paid my premium to the seller who took the risk. Since the index did not go up, I just lose the premium that I paid for owning the option. Because it is an index, I do not in fact buy or sell the actual stocks that make up the index. I am only dealing in money.

The index call seller is betting the other way. If the index goes up during the period of the option, this seller is liable for the increase. But if the index declines, he just keeps the premium he acquired in the sale.

4. INDEX PUT An index PUT gives the buyer the right

to collect a varying sum of money, until a specified time, as the index falls below a specific number. Thus, if I buy an index 300 PUT, and the index goes up, I lose my premium. If the index goes down, I make $100 for each point it goes down below 300 upon exercise or expiration. I can exercise my option at any time until it expires. If I wish, I can "close out" the position before it expires. If I own the position I can sell it at the market price, and if I have sold the position I can "buy it back" at market price at any time, unless market liquidity is affected by special events, as happened during the crash of 1987. Then you might not be able to buy or sell for some period of time.

The person on the other side of the trade, the seller of the index put, is in a reverse position (but with more risk, as we'll see below). This seller is liable for $100 for each point that the index declines below 300. If the index goes up, this seller just keeps the premium he collected from the sale.

5. STRIKE PRICE We have talked about the "strike price" in the previous examples. The "strike price" is either the dollar value of the stock, or the number (price level) of the index, specified in the option. Thus, in the examples above, when we talked about a Ford 35 CALL, the strike price is $35. When we talked about an index option at 300, the strike price is $300.

6. TERMINATION DATE. The "termination date" is the date on which, at the close of business, the option rights

Mervyn L. Hecht

FIGURE I-3   At-the-Money, In-the-Money, and
Out-of-the-Money CALLS and PUTS
on a $20 Stock.

AT-THE-MONEY; $20 STOCK PRICE

$20 CALL $20 PUT

IN-THE-MONEY; $20 STOCK PRICE

$30 PUT

$10 CALL

OUT-OF-THE-MONEY; $20 STOCK PRICE

$30 CALL

$10 PUT

expire unless exercised. Most options expire at the end of the third Friday of the designated month. Note that with the kinds of options we are mostly talking about in this book, you can exercise an option (or be put or called, if you are the seller) at any time during the life of the option - not only at the end of the period. (Some options only settle at the close). Also note that you may have to initiate some action through your broker, or else a long option may expire worthless even if it still has value!

7. AT-THE-MONEY. An option is "at-the-money" when the actual present dollar value or index number is the same as the strike price specified in the option. The option is "in-the-money" when the stock or index price goes past the strike price in the direction of profit for the holder; and the option is "out-of-the-money" when the current price is not yet at the strike price, in the direction of the loss for the holder. (These terms are illustrated in Figure I-3.)

8. COMBINATION. A "combination" is a strategy where more than one set of related option rights is held at the same time. A "spread" is a particular type of combination. In addition to spreads, one common combination for option traders is to buy or sell an out-of-the-money CALL and an out-of-the-money PUT on the same security at the same time. This combination is described in greater detail in Part IV below.

9. TIME VALUE PREMIUM "Time value premium" is

**FIGURE I-4   "Time Value Premium" (T.V.P.) for an
            Out-of-the Money CALL with a
            Strike Price of $30.**

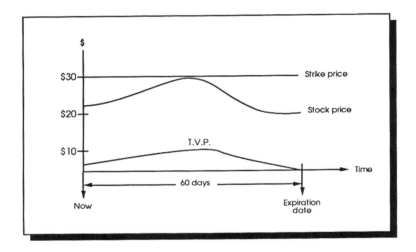

*The Time Value Premium goes up as the price of the stock gets
closer to the strike price ($30), but declines with time.*

the market value of the option excluding "intrinsic value." (Time Value Premium is illustrated in Figure I-4.) Time value premium is what the conservative option seller is trying to capture. Time value premium is really what the market thinks the underlying option rights for the future are worth. Thus, when an option is "out-of-the-money" the market price is 100% time value premium. This is covered in more detail below.

10. INTRINSIC VALUE. "Intrinsic value" is the amount of money, excluding "time value premium," which could be realized from the sale of an option at a specific point in time. (This is illustrated in Figure I-5.) Another way to look at intrinsic value is that it is the value than can be realized today, before any additional value is added for the possible profits in the future.

For example, if Ford Motor stock is at 35, and the 34 call is selling at $3, the intrinsic value is $1 and the time value premium is $2. This is because the owner of the call has a right to buy the stock at $1 below market value, but the option value is $2 higher than this price differential. If there is no other change in the market price, on the last day of the option, when there is no more "time value premium" because time has run out, the option will have a value of $1.

11. LONG AND SHORT. We speak of a holding as "long" when we own the position. To own a position means that you have purchased it, whether voluntarily or

FIGURE I-5   Intrinsic Value and Time Value Premium Components of the Price of an In-the-Money CALL Option.

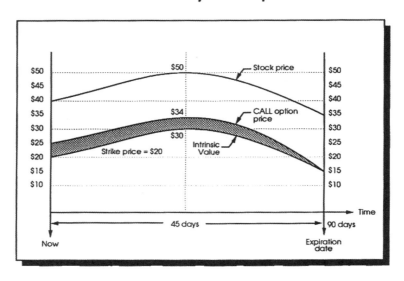

TODAY	IN 45 DAYS	IN 90 DAYS
INTRINSIC VALUE 20 (40–20)	*INTRINSIC VALUE 30 (50–20)*	*INTRINSIC VALUE 15 (35–20)*
T.V.P. = $5	*T.V.P. = $4*	*T.V.P. = $0*
TOTAL PRICE $25	*TOTAL PRICE $34*	*TOTAL PRICE $15*

The Time Value Premium shrinks with time, while the Intrinsic Value changes with the stock price. If the option were not so far In-the-money, the Time Value Premium would fluctuate more as the stock price approached the option strike price.

involuntarily. Accordingly, if you buy a Call you are long that Call. If you sell a Call, you are short that position., If I say "I am long the Ford 55's and short the Ford 50's," that means that I bought the Ford Calls at a strike price of 55, and sold the Ford calls with a strike price of $50. I would then have to specify the termination date to fully describe my position. If I also own the Ford stock, I can be described as "long Ford." If I own 1,000 shares I might describe it as "long 1,000 shares of Ford."

When you sell calls, such as the Ford 50's, we say that you are "short the Ford 50's." When you sell an option it is sometimes referred to as "writing" the option, and the seller is referred to as an "option writer."

12. COVERED, HEDGED, AND NAKED. These are three terms that are related, and are easier to learn if learned at the same time. "Naked" is easy if you know the other two terms: it means that the position is not "covered" or "hedged." For example, if you just sell a call, and you don't have any protection against the unlimited potential loss that will arise from an increase in the underlying stock, you hold that call "naked."

"Hedged" is a very broad term that includes the condition of being covered. Hedged just means "protected." Covering is one way to protect. If you sell a call, and you own 100 shares of the underlying stock, you are covered by the stock. That cover is a type of hedge. Another way to hedge your potential loss might be by buying a different call, creating a "spread"—something we will discuss below. Hedging is a very broad term, and includes some very imperfect hedging devices, such as holding stock in a different company within the same industry group.

D. Basic Examples

Now that I have listed the definitions of the key option terms for your reference, let us look at some examples. In these examples, I will alternatively use the pronouns "he" and "she" in describing the parties to the transaction, but there is no particular significance to either pronoun.

(1) The Stock CALL Purchase

The best known option is the stock CALL. One stock CALL gives the holder (the buyer) the right to buy 100 shares of the stock. For example, if IBM is $85 per share on October 15, you can expect to buy a January 90 IBM CALL for approximately $1.30. If you buy that CALL, since each CALL represents 100 shares, you will pay approximately $130 (plus between $25 and $50 in commission) and for that premium you will receive the right to buy 100 shares of IBM stock for $90 per share until the close of the business day of the third Friday in January.

Since the stock has not yet reached $90, the $1.30 that you are paying is strictly "on the come." Unless the stock goes over $90 a share, your option will expire worthless. The option is therefore "out-of-the-money." The strike price of the option would have to be below 85 in order for the option to be "in-the-money."   Since options are denominated in increments, usually of $5 or $10, the $80 strike price is the closest one that is "in-the-money." An 85 option would be "at-the-money."

Why would anyone buy a January 90 CALL on IBM? The buyer of that option may believe that there is a substantial likelihood that IBM stock will go over $92 by the expiration date. Note that the stock has to go to approximately $92 for the buyer to make any money. If the stock only goes to $91, the buyer can buy the stock for $90, and immediately sell it for $91, but the commissions and the cost of the option combined will be greater than the profit (depending, of course, on the number of options purchased and the commission cost per share). The point is that the buyer, in anticipating the profits of a Call purchase, must include the cost of the option and the commissions.

The buyer of an option like this has a somewhat different mind-set than the buyer of IBM stock. The buyer of the stock has a substantial sum of money to invest; in this case, 100 shares at $85 would be $8,500. Presumably the buyer of the stock is willing to invest that sum of money because he believes that the stock will rise in value at some time in the future, coupled with the potential for dividend income. The option buyer in this example is not willing to invest $8,500. Because the option buyer believes that he or she can predict the rise of the stock within a specified time period, and the prediction can be tested for a small amount of money (the cost of the option), the *buyer* is willing to risk $130.

As you will learn, below, however, it is likely that this option buyer has purchased the option as part of a more complex strategy, either to capture some portion of a premium, or to hedge a different position.

(2) The Stock CALL Sale

Now, let us look at the other side of that transaction, from the perspective of the person who <u>sold</u> the CALL that the buyer purchased. Perhaps at that moment IBM stock is not much in favor with the investment counselors and stock market pundits. The company has had disappointing earnings, and sales are not as strong as expected. Some say the whole computer industry is weakening. Competition by Compaq and Apple is strengthening. The seller doubts that IBM stock will reach $90 in the near future. He is therefore willing to sell one or more CALLS of IBM and collect $130 per CALL, less commissions. If, between mid-October and the end of next January, approximately 30 days, IBM stock does not go over $90, the seller of the CALL will keep the $130. If IBM goes over $90, the seller will be "called" and will have to deliver 100 shares of IBM in exchange for payment of $9,000, and in so doing will give back some or all of the $130. This "give back" might be by way of delivering stock that the seller already has, at a price below market value, or the seller may simply buy the stock at the market value (over $90) to make good delivery against the call.

If IBM goes over $91.30 the seller will lose $100 for each point that the stock exceeds this figure when the option is called. Note that the seller might be "called" before the expiration date, if IBM stock goes over $90 at any time before the expiration.

Why make this sale? Perhaps it is greed. Greed is a strong driving force in the stock market. The prospect of collecting an easy $130 is attractive. If you make that sale without an adequate information base about IBM stock, you are speculating. The speculation carries with it a theoretically infinite risk, since theoretically the stock could go up to any number. But, as a practical matter, even if you have no information about the stock, a Blue Chip stock like IBM is extremely unlikely to go up say, 50% in a 30 day period. So, while there is a theoretically unlimited risk that cannot be precisely defined, there are some practical limits on the "up side," which this trade involves. And, of course, the risk can be contained by various strategies, such as owning the underlying stock.

NOTE THAT THERE IS AN IMPORTANT DIFFER-ENCE BETWEEN THE BUYER OF THE CALL AND THE SELLER OF THE CALL. THE BUYER OF THE CALL RISKS ONLY THE PRICE OF THE OPTION. THE SELL-ER OF THE CALL RUNS A RISK WHICH IS NOT PRE-CISELY DEFINED.

(3) Stock Indexes

Options on a stock index are very different than stock options. Indexes on commodities or interest rate futures are again something very different.   To understand options on a stock index, it helps to first understand what a stock index is.

Many stock index options are written on an index that has "OEX" as its symbol. The proper name of this index is the "Standard & Poor 100 Index."   It is also commonly known as the "S&P 100."   Be careful not to confuse it with the "S&P 500," which is a more frequently quoted index.

The S&P 100 is a group of 100 allegedly market representative stocks selected by the Standard & Poor Company. In the old days the index that everyone heard about was the Dow Jones Industrial Average, based on 30 allegedly representative stocks widely quoted by news commentators. (See Figure 1-6.)   The S&P 100, which I will refer to in this book as the OEX, fluctuates, generally speaking, in parallel fashion with the Dow Jones Index. Because of the way the index is constructed, as a rule of thumb the Dow Jones Index moves 7 or 8 points for each 1 point of the OEX. So on a day when the news reporters say that the Dow Jones went up 22 points, I would expect the OEX to have moved up between 3 and 4 points. As I write this, the Dow Jones *is* fluctuating around 10,000, and the OEX is at approximately 1,100, so the ratio of the total is not 1:8, but the fluctuation is, roughly speaking.

Figure 1-6 Stocks Making up the
Dow Jones Industrial Average

Dow 30 Components

Company	Price
3M Corporation	80.95
Alcoa, Inc	33.61
Altria Group, Inc	58.05
American Express Company	55.70
American Intl Group, Inc.	61.80
Boeing Co.	53.77
Caterpillar, Inc.	90.18
Citigroup, Inc	45.15
E.I. du Pont de Nemours and Company	44.88
Exxon Mobil Corp.	50.38
General Electric Company	36.27
General Motors Corporation	38.90
Hewlett Packard Co	20.08
Honeywell Intl, Inc	35.46
IBM	94.45
Intel Corporation	24.16
J.P. Morgan & Co. Incorporated	37.42
Johnson & Johnson	60.54
McDonald's Corporation	29.30
Merck & Co., Inc.	27.12
Microsoft Corporation	26.86
Pfizer, inc.	27.23
SBC Communications, Inc.	25.89
The Coca-Cola Company	39.73
The Home Depot, Inc.	42.70
The Procter & Gamble Company	54.32
United Technologies Corporation	97.26
Verizon Communications	41.10
Wal-Mart Stores, inc	55.25
Walt Disney Company (The) (Holding Company)	26.66

But because there are different stocks in each index, sometimes they move quite differently.

The OEX is important to us in this discussion because it is an index on which many, if not most, index options are written. But there is a big difference between writing an option on an index and writing an option on a stock. If you buy an IBM Jan 100 Call before the option expiration date you can buy 100 shares of IBM stock for $100 a share. If you buy an OEX Jan 550 CALL, you can't buy the underlying stocks. If you exercise your option, which you would only do if the OEX goes over $550, all you get is money. This is a very big difference which is of particular importance when we compare the sale of a PUT on a stock and an index PUT. So, first, let us look at the purchase and sale of a stock PUT, and then come back to compare it with the purchase and sale of an index PUT.

(4) Stock PUTS

If I buy an IBM Jan 100 PUT when IBM stock is at $100, I can sell 100 shares of IBM, until the expiration of the PUT, at $100 per share. Obviously, if IBM goes down below $100 per share, it will pay me to sell it for $100, and buy it back at the open market at the lower price. If IBM stock goes down to $95 during my option period, I can buy 100 shares at $95 during my option period, then I can sell 100 shares at $100 by exercising my PUT option, and make a $500 profit before commission and the cost of the put. Assuming that I paid $2 per share for the PUT, or

$200 total, that is the maximum amount I can lose. I will lose the $200 PUT option price if the stock stays at $100 or goes over $100.

If, after adequate research, I felt fairly certain that IBM stock will go down significantly within the next 30 days, for a small amount of money (the cost of the PUT option), I will be able to profit from the decline. But more likely, the reason I would buy the put is to "hedge" a position I already have. In this case, if I own 100 shares of IBM stock, and it is at $100 per share, and I believe the stock is likely to go down in the near future, I can buy the PUT to protect against this decline. For the cost of the put for every dollar in value my stock goes down, I will make $1 on the put. It's very much like insurance.

Since for every buyer there is a seller, let us examine the seller's state of mind: The seller has concluded that either IBM is not likely to go below 100 during the next 30 days, or if it does it's a good buy at that price. If the seller is engaging in this transaction as an isolated transaction, the seller's motive in making the PUT sale is either to collect the premium, or to acquire the stock during a dip in price.

Again, while it is possible that the buyer or the seller is engaged in this transaction as an isolated transaction, it is probably part of some broader strategy, such as those discussed below.

(5) Index PUTS

As I explained above, the sale of an index PUT is very different from the sale of a stock PUT. The seller of an IBM 100 PUT has assumed the risk of being obligated to buy IBM stock at $100 per share. This seller may well believe that the purchase of IBM stock at $100 a share is a good investment for the future even if the stock does not go up in a short term. By collecting a $200 premium, this seller is really only committing to purchase IBM stock at a net price of $98 per share, the $100 price that it is put to him or her, less the $2 per share already received as a premium. If the investor would be willing to buy 100 shares of IBM stock for $98 per share anyway, there is no additional risk in selling this PUT.

But the seller of a PUT on the OEX cannot take possession of the underlying stocks. Consider the sale of 1 OEX PUT Jan 550. For each point that the OEX goes below $550 the investor has a loss, if put at that time, of $100 per point. A single day 100 point drop in the Dow Jones, of 12 or 15 point drop in the OEX is no longer uncommon. Therefore a $1,500 loss is easily within the realm of possibility. Many would say that taking the possibility of a $1,500—or even perhaps a $3,000 loss to collect a $200 premium is a risky, speculative investment. We will examine this at greater length in later discussions in this book.

The purchase of an index PUT is more like the pur-

chase of a stock PUT, but where the stock price can fluctuate from activities affecting that particular company, the
index is less susceptible to such changes because of the
leveling effect of the stock basket on which the index price
is based.   Even if one stock goes way up or way down,
the effect on the index will be muted.

(6) Index CALLS

The buyer or seller of an index CALL may or may not
be in a different position from the buyer or seller of a stock
CALL. Let's look at the case where the investor has a
large diversified portfolio, containing all or many of the
same stocks which make up the S&P 100 Index. If that
investor sells an out-of-the-money CALL on the index, the
risk factor is not very different from an investor with holdings in IBM who sells a CALL against the IBM holding.
The most significant difference is that the investor with the
specific stock, IBM in our example, may be required to
deliver the stock if the price of the stock goes above the
strike price. If the seller of the CALL sold the CALL in the
hopes that the stock would be called away at the strike
price, the investor selling the CALL against her stock portfolio accomplished a sale of the stock. This does not happen with the seller of an index CALL. The seller of the
CALL cannot deliver the underlying stocks at expiration.
But, if the investor has a number of stocks that have gone
up in value, those stocks can be sold to pay for the loss
from the sale of the CALL. So in this sense there may not
be much difference.

One significant difference, however, is that the seller of a stock CALL is subject to any unusual increase in the company represented by that particular stock. For example, if that particular stock suddenly becomes the target of a takeover offer, the stock can jump way up in value. This can be very costly to the CALL seller. This is less likely to happen on an index CALL, since it is comprised of many different stocks. From this point of view, the seller of the index CALL is in a more conservative position than the seller of a CALL on a particular stock if he does not own the underlying stock.

E. What is "Speculation?"

Now that we have reviewed the basic option strategies, and some examples of option buying and selling, we are ready to take a look at the definitions of "risk," "speculation," and my key term - "appropriate."

What do we really mean when we say that an investment is "risky" or "speculative?"

From one point of view all stock investments are risky and speculative. There have been massive frauds in some of the finest blue-chip companies which caused the stock to drop like a bomb. When I first wrote this there was some discussion of barring Northrop Corporation from doing business with the U.S. government! Do you remember the missing oil in the American Express tanks? Or the phony insurance policies at Equity Funding? And of course everyone in business has now heard of Enron and WorldCom.

Some stocks are riskier than others. Some of the new emerging bio-technology stocks seem unlikely to produce a profit unless and until they develop a product to sell. On the other hand, during some periods steel companies had trouble finding buyers for their product because of competitive pricing problems, while at the moment they are doing well.

As in many areas of life, it seems that the term "risky" is a matter of gray, not black and white. Stock ownership in general is perceived as less risky than option transactions because of the impermanence of options. Stocks that pay dividends can be considered a safer asset to hold, because the dividend acts as a hedge against inflation, and a bottom point for the decline of stock price (based on yield).

After quality dividend paying stocks, in order of increasing risk, come blue-chip non-dividend paying stocks. Owning these stocks, which have an unlimited time to increase in value, seems less risky than options, which have a limited life and decline in time value premium as the length of their life shortens.

But if this is true, what can we say about a short option position? As time passes, the premium shrinks, and the likelihood of a profit to the investor-seller increases! Is an option sale therefore less risky than owning a stock?

The strange thing is that theoretically the answer is probably "yes." A properly structured short option position is probably less likely to lose money than the outright purchase of a blue chip stock held for the same period of time.

Aye – there's the rub - the position has to be properly structured. *Some short option positions carry very large risk-to-reward ratios, and those are the ones that get into the kind of trouble that we read about.* Let us look at some comparisons:

Suppose IBM stock is $100 per share today, and, based upon lots of data, you draw two conclusions, first, that the stock is likely to go up and second, the worst case decline over the next 90 days is 20 points, bringing the price of the stock down to $80 - a 20% decline.

-If I buy 100 shares at $100, I pay $10,000 and my assumed "worst case" risk is $2,000. But I also have to factor in the cost of the use of the $10,000, and the receipt of dividends.

-If I buy one 90 day CALL at 100, perhaps I pay $400. My investment is $400 and my maximum loss is $400. My gain potential is the same as if I purchased the stock, during the 90 day period. Of course then I can purchase another call, and so forth, and it will be a long time before

I use up $10,000 in premiums!

-If I sell one 90 day PUT at 100, I will collect in approximately $400. My assumed "worst case" risk is $1,600 (a 20 point drop at $100 per point, less the $400 premium). I am 4 points better off than if I had bought the stock, since I've already made the same profit as if the stock had gone up 4 points. And I didn't tie up $10,000, assuming that I had sufficient collateral already in the account to meet the broker's requirements.

So the potential dollar loss in this example is greater from the outright stock purchase than the call purchase, equal or so to the PUT sale, and the lowest is the purchase of the CALL. From one point of view, the stock purchase is the most risky.

So which strategy is the most risky? I don't know. It is a problem of definition, and point of view.

The point is that "risky" is not a very useful term for describing a market strategy. It is too broad and too general. What is important is to KNOW YOUR RISK. Option investors get into trouble when they engage in strategies not fully understood by them. That results in unexpected loss. Let me give you an example:

Mrs. Krinsky had purchased lots of stocks throughout the years. Then her broker told her about options. "A wonderful thing" he explained. "You go short 10 PUTS and collect $1,000 immediate profit with low risk. All you need is $10,000 in back-up money."

The broker was correct. He was selling way-out-of-the-money PUTS on a blue chip stock, and the risk of the stock declining, based on an historical analysis, was very small. Mrs. Krinsky, with a net worth of several hundred thousand dollars, thought of the transaction as a purchase for $10,000. If everything went wrong (not likely) she might lose her $10,000 "risk" money. But for $1,000 profit every 60 or 90 days that seemed reasonable. But the unlikely risk materialized. The stock dropped to a new 20 year low. There was a $25,000 loss. Mrs. Krinsky was shocked. She understood the concept of risk. What she did not understand was the EXTENT OF THE RISK. This misunderstanding led to an unpleasant lawsuit.

Maybe "speculative" means something different to investors than "risky." We all take risks (driving on the Los Angeles freeways, for example) and the concept of risk is endemic in the concept of investment. But none of us has to "speculate." That smacks of improper trading in pork bellies, or silver futures, and 1870's men in stovepipe hats earning large fortunes.

Yet it must mean something important. I note that several brokerage houses list "speculative" as one of the investment goal choices in the customer application form, sometimes automatically applied to uncovered option writing.

Do many customers invest with a goal to "speculate?" I doubt it. I think the brokerage house legal counsel put that choice there for their own protection, so option writers who later complain can be shrugged off as "speculators." Yet I have seen many option trades that one can only describe as speculative: close-to-the-money short combinations on relatively volatile stock, written repeatedly for the large premium income such high risk positions pay, where anyone should have expected an eventual big negative hit, wiping out all the premium income and then some.

In the long run, I suspect that the term "speculative" is just used to identify trades that the user of the term believes subject the investor to a high likelihood of loss. But the term is not used carefully and the usage has therefore carried over to whole categories. Because of the lack of precision in this usage, this term is also not very useful. For all these reasons, I suggest avoiding these terms altogether, and talk instead about the "appropriateness" of a trade for a particular investor. In addition to avoiding the looseness of the other terms, this term takes into consideration the financial position of the investor, psychological considerations, broker expertise, and risk-reward relationships - concepts usually not considered in a "risk" or "speculative" analysis. One might say that this term is subjective in nature, but I don't think so. I think there are a number of elements that can be identified and quantified so as to give a numeric ranking to an options customer which would identify the types of option strategies which that customer should do. This is what the options suitability forms used by brokerage houses are supposed to do, but they are woefully inadequate.

I do not use the term "suitability," although it is close in meaning, because it carries with it certain legal connotations which may not be synonymous with good judgment. Some strategies which are suitable under the law are used with poor judgment, and are not appropriate.

In this book, then, I speak of the appropriateness of various strategies and trades for various investors. When I speak of a "conservative strategy," I mean one which is appropriate to a conservative investor. By "conservative investor," I mean one who is primarily interested in conserving capital, in an inflation prone economy, and earning reasonable income with very low risk of capital erosion. That is my self-image and that is the person (directly or through his or her advisor) to whom much of this book is addressed.

When I speak of the "conservative investor," I also consider another characteristic. To my way of thinking, anyone who tries to make money in the stock market by predicting the likelihood of a rise and fall in stock prices, gold prices, or interest rates, is speculating. While I have the utmost respect for many researchers and economists, I have never seen any statistics which show a correlation between intelligence and the ability to predict the stock market, or between educational background in the field of economics and the ability to predict the future of interest rates.

Absent such statistics I have come to the conclusion that the conservative way to trade options is to take "neutral" positions which do not primarily depend for profitability upon a prediction of a future price change. The best way that I have found to do this is by capturing option premiums through the sale of options. Capturing option premiums really puts the investor into a position much like that of an insurance company. Nobody thinks that insurance companies are risky and everyone considers the insurance industry very conservative. Thus, if I can be like an insurance company, and take a certain amount of controlled risk in exchange for which people will pay me premiums, I will be a conservative investor.

And so, when I speak of option strategies for conservative investors, that is what I am referring to. Certain strategies discussed in sections II, III, and IV in this book are strategies appropriate for conservative investors, since they are designed to capture option premiums in positions where the risk is controlled. To better understand this concept, let us compare the relative positions of the buyer and the seller of an IBM 100 CALL to see if we can understand which one is taking the greater risk.

Clearly, both parties are speculating if they have not carefully investigated the appropriate financial data about IBM. Buying or selling any financial investment without knowing quite a bit about it (or relying on trustworthy information from a knowledgeable party) is just a gamble. So, let us assume that both parties are knowledgeable about the prospects of IBM, but that reasonable investors could hold varying opinions as to what the stock will do within the next 30 days.

Since option rights lose time value each day until they expire, the buyer has paid a premium for an asset that decreases in value each day that the expiration date draws nearer, unless the stock price goes up over the strike price. (See Figure I-7.) The seller, meanwhile, has collected a premium that can be invested in something else, including an interest bearing security, during the option period. The buyer is relying on his or her ability to predict a stock price fluctuation in order to make a profit. The seller is in a more neutral position; she need only hold the opinion that lack of volatility of the stock price is likely, in order to conclude that the trade is worthwhile.

One might say that the option buyer is engaged in a more risky transaction than the buyer of the underlying stock itself because of the short time period obtained through the option. But looking at it from a different point of view, one could say that because of the large investment required to buy the stock, the buyer of the stock is risking more money, and is more likely to lose because of the loss of the use of the funds for a long period of time during which the stock is held.

FIGURE I-7 Erosion of Time Value Premium Over Time.

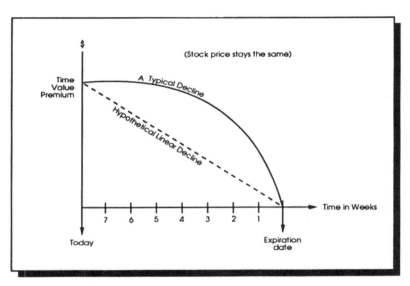

WEEKS TO EXPIRATION	HYPOTHETICAL VALUE	TYPICAL VALUE
8 =	1.0	1.0
7 =	0.87	0.93
6 =	0.75	0.85
5 =	0.62	0.79
4 =	0.5	0.71
3 =	0.375	0.61
2 =	0.25	0.50
1 =	0.12	0.36
0 =	0	0

To my way of thinking, whether or not the option buyer is speculating depends on (1) the relative amount of money spent by the buyer to acquire the option, compared to the buyer's total investment portfolio; and (2) whether or not the information obtained by the buyer was reasonably sufficient to conclude that the stock was likely to go up an appropriate amount before the expiration date. In other words, if the buyer acted reasonably, the trade is reasonable, and if the buyer acted unreasonably, the buyer is speculating just like the buyer who buys a stock with inadequate knowledge.

Now, let us look at the question of speculation from the seller's point of view. The seller is typically thought to have engaged in a high risk transaction because of the theoretically unlimited risk incurred.   As already explained, the risk is not really unlimited. There is some dollar figure which everyone could agree is beyond the realm of any reasonable likelihood for the stock to go to. No one would think it is possible for IBM stock to go from $100 to $300 in a 30 day period. There are, of course recent examples of takeovers where stock has gone up 20-40% in a matter of weeks. Some stocks have a much higher intrinsic value, realized on liquidation of the company's assets, than is reflected in the price of the stock in the open market. But that theoretical "takeover price" can be computed. So, again, I believe that whether or not the seller of this CALL engaged in a risky trade depends on the information available to the seller in determining the likelihood of the stock going up more than an expected amount in the following 30 day period. Additionally, the seller's ability to absorb loss is an important factor.

There is one more element which should be considered concerning risk in this transaction. For the seller the cost to hedge against a large loss is relatively small. To hedge the sale of a 100 CALL, if the stock is, say, $95, one can buy a CALL 10 or 15 points above the strike price of the short position (here, over 100 - say the 110 or 115) for a relatively small premium, and thereby be in a clearly defined risk position. This "spread" strategy is explained further in this book.

From a conservative investment point of view - and clearly from a litigation point of view, it is very difficult to justify the failure of a seller to hedge such a short position, when it can be done for a reasonably small price.

What can we say in conclusion? Any investment, if not well thought out and researched, should be considered risky and inappropriate. Investments which can result in a loss beyond the financial resources of the investor's risk capital are inappropriate for that investor. Using options as an investment resource can reduce the risk of many investments. Some option strategies are conservative in nature, and can produce or enhance income with little risk. It is those strategies to which this book is devoted.

F. How to Enter an Order

All exchange traded options are settled through the Options Clearing Corporation, sometimes called the "OCC." This clearing house, comprising well capitalized brokers, guarantees each option transaction. Once an option trade has been settled on the floor of an exchange, the parties no longer look to each other for delivery and payment, but look to the OCC. Thus, the OCC becomes the buyer to every seller and the seller to every buyer.

Every purchase of an option contract from someone is offset by a sale by someone else. But all option transactions go through the OCC, which acts as a middleman for the transaction, and thus removes the credit risk inherent in the old "over-the-counter" market. There is also more liquidity, since a market maker is required to buy all options offered for sale.

A market maker is a person who quotes a bid and ask price for an option whenever asked to do so. The "bid" is the buy price, and the "ask" is the sell price. Market makers do not handle public orders; they buy and sell for their own accounts only.

A customer wishing to buy or sell options must contact a broker, who relays the order to a floor broker for execution. The floor broker deals with the market maker. An order book official, known as a "board broker," keeps a record of unfilled limit orders, that is, an order to buy or sell at a specified price (the "limit") or better. Information on all outstanding limit orders is available to all traders. This system is in contrast to the system of specialists who make a market in particular stocks on the listed stock exchanges, and who also keep the book, but do not reveal that information to other traders. The CBOE claims that the use of board brokers leads to more efficient trading. Not every option exchange uses the board broker system.

There are two kinds of orders in general use with options. The most common is the "market order," a simple order to buy or sell an option at the best possible price as soon as the order gets to the exchange floor. While this is the most simple and most common, I do not recommend it. I recommend a "limit order," an order to buy or sell at a specified price or better. I decide in advance at what price I am willing to buy or sell. I tell the broker that price. If the order goes through, good. If not, the broker calls me back and tells me why, and what the current price is.

Some traders use a "good till canceled" order. This means that the order remains in effect until it is specifically canceled. I suggest against this kind of order. Options are too volatile, and the memory too short, to have an order outstanding for an infinite period of time. I recommend, at the most, placing an order that is good until the close of the business day. Then you can look at it again the next day and decided if you want to put it on again or not.

Finally, when entering an option trade with more than one position included, such as a spread, it is advisable to include an instruction of "all or none," which means that all the positions, or none of them, should be executed. Along the same lines, when entering an order for a spread or combination it is best to specify a combined net credit or debit. For example, if trying to buy a call at $2, and selling a put at $1, put in the order "all or none for a net debit of not over $1."

There are many different kinds of orders, most of which I am not going to describe here. Let me just tell you in summary what I do when I enter an order:

1. I decide in advance at what price I am willing to buy or sell. If the order goes through, good. If not the broker calls me back and tells me why, and what the current price is. I almost <u>never</u> give a "market" order, that is, an OK to buy or sell at the going price, whatever it is.

2. I never give a "good till canceled" order. I always limit the order to the end of the day.

3. When appropriate, I leave instructions with the broker to take certain actions if a particular event occurs. For example - "If Ford goes down to $40, close out the positions."

4. Finally, if I'm entering an order with two or more related positions, such as a spread, I tell the broker to

make it "all or none," which means place all of the positions simultaneously, or none of them.

G. Option symbols.

Option symbols generally follow a very logical pattern. You take the underlying stock symbol, such as "DD" for E.I. Du Pont de Nemours & Co. Then you add two letters, one for the month, and one for the strike price. The letters are different for puts than for CALLS. For CALLS the lettering system for the months begins, reasonably enough, with "A." So January is A, February is B, etc. The strike price letter is a bit more difficult to figure out, because some stocks have strike prices every $5, and some every $10. Du Pont has $5 spreads for its strike prices, so the Jan 45 call is DDAI. I is the 9th letter of the alphabet, and 45 is the 9th digit in a series of counting by 5. A January 5 call would end in AA.

Many—probably most—options are not available for each month; they trade in cycles. Some are two month cycles, and some three month cycles. Leaps (see below) are one year options. So if you see a call available for January, you may not see one for February or March, and the next one might be in May. And they only go out a certain length of time, usually less than one year. And when a stock is moving up or down quickly, options near the current price may or may not be available for a while, until the market catches up or the price stabilizes. So if you think you can just find a call above the market price any

time you want to, think again. Many a broker has made
that mistake of judgment.

There are, unfortunately, a number of exceptions to the
general rules of symbol assignment, which require the
exchanges to assign different symbols in special cases.
A common example is where there is a stock split.
Another is where there is a merger. When there is a stock
split, there may be two series of options outstanding at
the same time on the same company, one based on the
original stock price, and the other on the new price. Or
the option price to which the old symbol relates may just
be changed. Where there is a merger, there typically are
two option series outstanding at the same time, one relat-
ing to the "old" company, and the other to the "new" company. There are other situations where two or more
series of options are outstanding at the same time, and
special symbols are utilized. Be careful.

PART II - Basic Strategies

A. Buying an Option
[NOT recommended by itself]

The most simple option strategy is just to buy an option. You can buy either a PUT or a CALL. Whichever you buy, your risk is limited to the amount that you pay to buy the option.

When you buy a Call, it gives you the right to BUY the underlying stock. So, if you buy 1 IBM March 85 Call, you have the right to buy 100 shares of IBM stock for $85 per share until the third Friday of March. If you pay $2 for the Call, it means $2 per share, or $200 per option (which represents 100 shares). In this scenario, the stock has to move up to over 87 for you to make a profit. But you would exercise the Call at any price over 85, just before the termination date, to recoup some of your cost. Obviously the purchase of a Call, by itself, is for someone that wants to be in the position of owning 100 shares of stock for a short period of time, without putting up all the money necessary for such a purchase.

The purchase of a Put gives you the right to SELL 100 shares of the stock at the strike price to the termination date. For example, if you buy 1 IBM 85 March Put, you have the right to sell 100 shares of IBM at $85 through the third Friday of March. Note that you do not have to own the 100 shares that you might sell. You could always buy the 100 shares at the same time you sell them. On the third Friday of March, if IBM is at $80, you can buy 100 shares for $8,000, and simultaneously sell them (by "putting" them to the person who sold the Put) for $8,500. Or, at any time during the life of the option, you could just sell the option for its market price. Once IBM stock drops below $85, the market price for the 85 Put option will be considerably higher than it was when the stock was at or over $85 per share.

Purchasing a Put can be viewed in several ways. For some investors it is a way to profit from an anticipated drop in stock price. For others it is like buying an insurance policy. If you own 100 shares of IBM stock, and some event is about to happen that might adversely affect the price, or you plan to sell and want to defer the sale while not risking a drop in price, buying a Put can protect you against a decline in value of your holding.

When you buy an option, your only risk is that you will lose the premium that you paid. If you pay very little for it, and you have reasonable grounds to believe that you might make a profit, it could be a reasonable investment, and not very "risky," since you haven't put much money at risk. I think some people confuse "risky" with "wasteful." There is a certain element to the puritan ethic which considers it wasteful to buy something impermanent. Thus, it seems to some to be a waste of money to spend on food or entertainment. But buying a sturdy piece of furniture would not be wasteful.

And so it is, to some, with buying an option. If you save up your money and buy a share of stock instead, you have something of permanence. But if you buy the option, it expires.

To me, "risky" means that you are put in a position where there is a significant likelihood of losing an inappropriate sum of money. Therefore, buying an option, by my definition, is rarely risky. It may be stupid. It may be wasteful. It may be inappropriate. But it's rarely risky, because you know the cost at the outset, and that is what you can lose.

The main reason investors buy an option by itself is for leverage. If you believe that IBM stock will go up from 100 to 110 in the next 30 days, to buy 1000 shares would require that you put up $100,000 (or perhaps half of that if you buy on margin). But you can control 1000 shares, and be in the same position *vis-à-vis* the right to a gain on the increase, if you buy 10 calls. To buy 10 calls will only require a cash outlay of, perhaps $2,000.

In my opinion, however, buying an option is usually only

worthwhile if it is part of a larger strategy, such as using this purchase as a hedge against accepting too much risk. You will see examples of this when we discuss spreads below. To buy an option by itself and make money on it requires a correct judgment about a stock price change in a short period of time. Except where you have special information about a company, I have usually not found this to be successful, especially after transaction costs.

Thus, in the IBM example above, unless IBM stock in fact goes over 87 within the following 30 days, you will lose money. If it should go to 94 during that period of time, you will make a $7,000 profit (less transaction costs). If you can double your money in a 30 day period it certainly is a good result. Personally, however, I have not been able to consistently predict stock prices over a short period of time well enough to benefit from this strategy.

B. Selling an Option

The next simplest strategy is to sell an option. But this is quite a bit more complicated than buying an option.

First of all, when you sell an option there is a big difference between selling an in-the-money option and selling an out-of-the-money option.   Selling an in-the-money option subjects you to much higher risk than selling an out-of-the-money option. Selling a long-term option usually brings in a much higher premium than selling a short-term option. But selling any option, <u>by itself</u>, generally subjects you to a very substantial market risk. For this reason, there are very few cases where it would be appropriate for an investor to just sell a Call or (to a lesser extent—see below,) a Put, except where the sale is part of a larger strategy. Absent the ability to absorb the worst case risk, and absent extremely unusual and dependable information, this is the one area of option trading which is most likely to be inappropriate for most investors.

Why does the sale of an in-the-money Call put the seller at greater market risk than the sale of an out-of-the-money Call? Take a look at Figure II-1. The seller of the out-of-the-money Call has a window of stock price volatility before the risk of loss materializes -i.e., the price increases to the strike price. But the seller of the in-the-money (or at-the-money) Call is subjected to loss point-for-point with a rise in the stock price.

Because the sale of an in-the-money Call can produce a large cash influx into your account (the intrinsic value), one sometimes sees brokers selling them to cover up losses. The cash premium inflates the cash position in the account, although if the option is priced on the statement it reduces the account value. But in-the-money options usually have a lower time value premium component, and are therefore less valuable as a way to collect premium income. And premium income is what you can profit from, not cash from intrinsic value. Cash collected

FIGURE II-1 Comparing Risk of Sale of an In-the-Money CALL with an Out-of-the-Money CALL

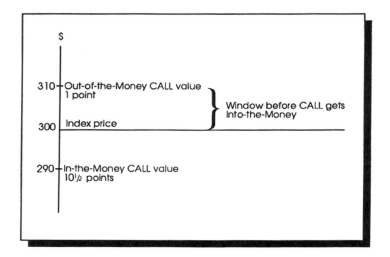

The index is at 300 on this chart. If you sell a 310 call, the price might be 1 or 2 points, depending on the volatility of the stock – or less if there is low volatility. the index has to move up 10 points, or approximately 3%, before you start to lose money. This is an out-of-the money call, and the premium is all based on risk.

If you sell a 290 call, it is in-the-money. The price wil be over $10 of intrinsic value. The right to buy something at $290 when there is a market value of $300 is always worth at least $10. In this case the risk of profit or loss is much greater than in the out-of-the-money call because the value will change dollar-for-dollar with the stock price. Since most stock prices change at least weekly, there will regularly be changes in the call value.

How to Make Money with Stock Options   61

from a sale with intrinsic value is just trading risk for cash on a temporary basis.

As far as I know, there is rarely a valid reason for you yourself, or you on behalf of someone to whom you owe a fiduciary duty, to sell an uncovered call solely in the expectation of making a profit from that single position. That is because there is, in every case that I can think of, a way to hedge the risk for a nominal sum, without interfering with the primary motive of potentially profiting from the sale of the Call option. Since there is always some combination strategy which will work almost as well as the individual option sale, it seems to me generally inappropriate to engage in the simple sale of an option - except in one situation - the uncovered Put.

Under proper circumstances, selling an uncovered Put is a more conservative investment strategy than buying and holding stock.

Suppose, for example, that I would be willing (and am financially able) to buy 100 shares of IBM at $80. But the stock is now at $90. At 90 I don't dislike it, but I don't love it. At $80 I love it, and I want it.   So I sell the 90 day 85 PUTS at, say, 3 points (or I sell the 95 PUTS at say, 6 points if I really want the stock.) This means I agree to buy the stock at the strike price (85) at any time during the option period, because my net cost, with the premium I receive, is a price I am willing to pay. In the case of the 85 Put with a $3 premium, that price would be $82. If I can get a $7 premium for the 95 in-the-money Put, my cost will be $88.00.

At expiration, if the stock has remained above my strike price, I keep the earned premium I received, and I rewrite a new position. I keep rewriting until either (1) the stock dips to my strike price, and I acquire it, (2) it rises beyond the point where there is any significant premium in the 85 PUT (or maybe I roll up to a higher strike price), or (3) I have made so much premium income writing these Puts that I retire from the market. (See Figure II-2).

Any of these alternatives is not bad. The only negative is that if IBM moves up to $250 and never dips, I will kick myself for having written Puts instead of buying the stock. But my billfold, swollen from profits from Put premiums, will shelter the blow!

Writing Puts in situations where the investor is willing and able to take delivery of the underlying stock is a sound conservative strategy. The main caveat is to be sure that you have enough money on hand to buy the stock if that becomes the result of the strategy.

One appropriate use of the Call option sale is the <u>sale of an in-the-money Call to hedge a long in-the-money PUT position</u>. (This is a good example of how option strategies can get complicated, but if you take your time and diagram out the positions you will come to an understanding of how it works).

**FIGURE II-2   Selling a PUT as a Method of Acquiring
Stock.**

STARTING POSITION

```
 $
110    Stock at $109 ──────────────────────
105    Sell 105 PUT for $3  ─ ─ ─ ─ ─ ─ ─ ─ ─ ─
100
 95
```

AT EXPIRATION:

*If the stock stays at $109, I keep $300 PUT premium and write
another PUT. If stock is below $105 (for example $104) I will be
PUT the stock at $105 less the $3 premium received for a net cost
of $102 per share. That means that I am obligated to buy 100
shares of the stock, for a net cost of $10,200,*

An example: when X stock is at $100, I sell a $95 PUT for $3 (yielding a total of $300 less commissions) in the hope of acquiring 100 shares of the stock at $92 net per share if X dips below $95. I expect to be put the stock, that is, to be forced to buy the stock at $95, if the stock price falls below $95 during the option period. If the price stays above $95 I will just keep the $300 premium.

My only risk of loss in this transaction is a drop in the stock price below $92. If the stock was to drop precipitously down to, say, $80, and I was forced to buy it at $95, I would immediately have an unrealized loss of $1,500, less the $300 premium, or $1,200. This is "sold low, bought high."

To protect against this, if the stock drops to $91 I can sell an in-the-money Call at a strike price of 85 for perhaps as much as $9—to pick a number for illustration purposes, and collect $900. (Call prices become inflated when the stock becomes volatile - this $900 in premium consists of $600 of intrinsic value and $300 of premium value - See Figure I-5). If the stock price stays at 91 until expiration, I will acquire the stock at $95 per share. I collected $300 from the original PUT, and, after paying out $600 (91 less 85—repaying the intrinsic value), the Call will make another $300 profit for a net stock price of $89 ($95 less $600 net in premium). I will have converted a prospective $100 loss on my original Put position (95 less 91 was a $400 loss less the $300 collected in premiums) to a $200 profit: I was hoping to acquire the 100 shares of stock for a net $9,100 and in fact acquired it for $8,900. See Figure II-3.

At the same time, the Call acted as a hedge.   The hedge feature works as follows:

If the stock price moves up after my sale of the Call, I will lose $100 per point on the Call, but make $100 per point on the put, (up to a $95 stock price), which is now in-the-money. So I am "hedged," or neutral, when the stock moves in the range of 85 to 95.

If the stock price continues to deteriorate, which is the risk I am hedging against by selling the in-the-money Call, I will continue to lose $1 per point on the Put, but make $100 on the call (down to $85).   By selling the Call I stopped my downside risk between a drop in the stock price from $91 to $85. If the stock continues to fall below $85, I can sell another in-the-money Call and repeat the process. (See Figure II-2).

The calculation looks like this:

Premiums Received:

Sale of PUT	$ 300
Sale of CALL	1,000
Total premiums received	1,300

FIGURE II-3 Use of an In-the-Money CALL as a Hedge for an Out-of-the Money PUT That Went In-the-Money

STARTING POSITION

$		
100	Stock Price = $100	Out-of-the-Money
95	Sale of Out-of-the-Money PUT	window
	60 days @ $2	(95–100)
90		
85		

POSITION AFTER 30 DAYS
STOCK DROPS TO $91.00

$		
100		PUT $4 In-the-Money
95	$95 PUT strike price	
90	$91 stock price	CALL $6 In-the-Money
85	Sell new 85 CALL @ $9	By selling this CALL I hedge against further loss, and pick up additional Time Value Premium.

POSITION AT EXPIRATION (60 DAYS)
STOCK STAYS AT $91.00

$	
100	
95	PUT - expires and I am put the stock at 95
90	Stock still at $91
85	CALL expires @ $6

By selling the CALL I picked up $3 of Time Value Premium. Added to the $2 received on the original sale of the PUT, I have received $500 in premium. I own the stock at $95, and the stock is worth $91 — so I could sell out and approximately break even on the transaction. While the goal was not to break even, that's not a bad result for a stock that fe

Buy back the call when the stock ends

the period at $91 per share: - 600

Net premium received $ 700

Cost of stock $9,500

NET COST $8,800

I started out hoping to pay $92.00 for 100 shares of IBM stock if it dipped below $95. By selling a rich Call after the stock dropped below my expectations, I improved my position by $400 at a low risk. This is why options are so wonderful. But note that this strategy works because I took advantage of movement in the stock price. That is where option strategies can be most useful as protective devices.

C. The Buy-Write [Strongly recommended]

One of the most common institutional options trades is the "buy-write." In this trade, the investor buys a stock and writes a Call against the stock. (See Figure II-4.) Absent some special strategy, the Call is typically 5-10% out-of-the-money. Let's look at an example:

FIGURE II-4 The Buy-Write Strategy.

STARTING POSITION

```
$
120
110   Sell 10 CALLS @ 110 for $2
100   Buy 1,000 shares @ $100
 90
```

At Expiration

If stock is over $110:

Called away for:	*$110,000*
Cost was:	*100,000*
Profit of:	*10,000*
Plus premium:	*2,000*
TOTAL PROFIT ·	*$12,000*

*PLUS ANY DIVIDENDS
BEFORE THE STOCK
WAS CALLED AWAY.*

If stock is under $110:

*Received $2,000 premium
and dividends.*

On January 20 I buy 1,000 shares of IBM at $100 a share, investing $100,000. Simultaneously I sell 10 CALLS of the April 110's for two points, taking in $2,000 of premium. Now my net cost per share is only $98. If IBM stock goes over $110 during the following 90 days, absent some action on my part, it will be called away from me (that is, sold to the owner of the Call) at $110. So there are three possibilities:

(1) IBM stock goes down. In this case I keep the premium, and I am more than $2,000 better off than had I just bought the stock. Obviously, if I intended to buy IBM stock anyway, selling the Call was a good move.

(2) IBM stock does not fluctuate very much during the 90 day period. Again, I keep the $2,000 premium, and, coupled with the quarterly dividend of just under 1% per annum, I have increased my yield approximately 8% annualized. I get that figure by taking $2,000/100,000 for 1/4th of the year, or 2% times 4.

(3) IBM stock goes over $110 during the 3 month period. If I allow the stock to be called away (without buying other stock to deliver), I will make a $10,000 capital gain, plus the $2,000 premium, plus any dividend declared during this period. My annualized return will be approximately 30%!

Of course, I can't always get 2 points for a call 10% out of the money on a stock like IBM, and it is a stretch to write it exactly four times in one year. But you get the idea.

What I gave away was the potential for a really large profit in the IBM stock during the 90 day period. For this reason, the buy-write strategy is not appropriate for those who want to get rich quickly. It's best for those who want to enhance their returns on stock.

If the stock goes over $110 and I don't want to sell the stock, I can buy back the Calls (at a loss) at any time. Of course, the loss is offset by the unrealized gain in the stock price. Or, I can buy back those Calls and sell other Calls at a higher strike price and in a different time frame. These are "rolling" strategies which are described in greater detail in the text below.

D. Summary of Simple Strategies

The simplest strategy in options is to buy an option. But experts in the market will tell you that most people who buy an option lose money on it. Some say that since there are two sides to every trade, there must be an even number that make money and lose money. But with commissions, that's clearly not true: the sellers have the advantage. Certainly in many cases the option buyer hopes to lose money on an option, since the option is purchased as a hedge for some other kind of position, and that position makes a large profit which is only slightly reduced by the cost of the option. That's like life insurance—I hope to lose the premium every time I pay it!

I believe that most sophisticated investors will agree, however, that merely buying a Put or a Call for the purpose of expecting it to go up in value is rarely a good investment. Naturally, there are special circumstances where the investor has a strong basis for believing that there will be a substantial short term movement in a particular stock or in the market as a whole. In these circumstances the purchase of an option makes sense. In such a situation, the purchase of an option with a risk of loss appropriate for the investor should not be considered as a risky investment, because the risk of loss is limited to the cost of the investment, and therefore can be carefully evaluated by the investor at the initiation of the investment.

The other side of that transaction is to sell an option. Selling a Call, by itself, without being hedged or as part of a combination, puts the seller at the risk of a loss which is usually very large compared to the potential profit. Even a non-volatile stock may be subject to a takeover, can have a very substantial increase in a short period of time, and can therefore subject the naked Call seller to great risk.

The seller of a naked Put on any stock, no matter how highly valued for stability, subjects the seller to a substantial risk, since adverse news or information about the company or industry can cause a substantial decline in the value of any stock. Who could have predicted the uncovering of massive fraud either in the Equity Funding

Corporation or the Technical Equity Companies; the American Express scandal or the LTV bankruptcy" What about Enron, Tyco and WorldCom?   But to write (sell) a naked stock Put is a very conservative move <u>as a method of capturing ownership of a stock during a decline</u>, at a price reduced by the premium.

The buy-write is a widely used method of increasing the current income from stock holdings, while giving up only some portion of the upside potential. This technique is a low risk option technique, provided that the investor has already decided to accept the risk of holding the stock. A large capital investment is required to participate in a buy-write, and that is its main drawback. For this reason, this strategy is often favored by institutional investors that have the capital available for wide diversification. There are also potential tax drawbacks which are discussed below under "tax considerations."

The basic option strategies that I consider often inappropriate for the conservative investor are the following:

1. Selling an uncovered stock Call.

2. Selling more uncovered stock Puts than you are prepared to convert to long term stock holdings if the stock is put to you.

3. Selling any uncovered index option that is not part of a hedged strategy.

The following basic strategies stand out as those used regularly by professionals to make money in the options market:

1. Acquiring stock at a discount, or during a price dip, by selling Puts.

2. Selling out-of-the-money Calls against stocks owned, to generate premium income. When the stock is purchased at the same time the Calls are written, this is called a "buy-write."

E. Basic Principles of Conservative Option Strategies

This Book is really two books rolled into one: the "how to" explanations, and a philosophical discussion of stock market strategies. As with any philosophy, the one expressed here has a certain number of underlying assumptions. Since we have been engrossed in a lot of "how to" discussion, it is now time to look at the philosophical part and, particularly, some of these underlying assumptions.

Some of the assumptions are pretty obvious. Investors want to make the best return on their investment commensurate with the degree and dollar amount of risk they are willing to take. In other words, if I can get $3 by investing $1 it is better than if I can only get $2 by investing the same $1, provided that the risk is the same.

Some of the assumptions in this book are less obvious. I don't think anybody can predict the market with
much success. Some people are pretty good at particular stocks, where they either have an inside track on
the company, or are willing to devote an extraordinary
amount of time and energy to gathering and analyzing
information about the company. That's not me. But I do
think that one can predict a range of fluctuations in the
market with some degree of statistical probability. While
there are periods of unusual volatility both in particular
stocks and the overall market, this is not true most of the
time, and most weeks that go by the market does not
move more than one would anticipate from looking at
past performance.

Since I wrote the first edition of this book there has
been some very interesting theoretical research in
financial markets. The International Herald Tribune, on
June 19, 2004, ran an article by James K. Glassman
about a new book authored by Nassim Nicholas Taleb.
The name of the book is "Fooled by Randomness," and
the thesis seems to be that market movement is
random, and therefore cannot be predicted from either
the past or from data. This might be a somewhat
extreme position.

But along the same lines is a book by Benoit
Mandelbrot and Richard L. Hudson, named "The
(mis)behavior of markets. " Mandelbrot is the famous
mathematician who "invented" fractal theory," which in

turn begot "chaos theory." I've heard that there is a lot of money going into research in an attempt to apply chaos theory to analysis and prediction of financial markets. Mandelbrot's thesis is too complex to summarize in a few sentences, but one part of it rings a bell with those of us who are sailors. When we prepare for an offshore cruise, we prepare for the worst possible scenario. Even if there hasn't been a hurricane off the coast of California for 50 years, and even if we plan to be offshore for only a couple of days, we (1) take food and water for at least one week, (2) have rigging strong enough to withstand a hurricane, and (3) take survival gear in case everything else goes wrong.

We do that for sailing. But we rarely do that in investing. Mandelbrot points out that markets are not rational, and do not follow "common sense" or what we would normally expect them to do, and are more volatile that we commonly perceive them to be.

I think that it is pretty reasonable to infer some basic principles from these underlying assumptions:

1. First of all, for short term investment it is cheaper and safer to buy Calls than to buy stock. Yet I never do it. Why not" Because I never think of myself as a short term investor in stocks. I always think of myself as a long term investor in stocks.

But, historically I know that is not true. Typically I

own stocks for one or two years, and then I am out of that company and into some other one. Typically I am into different industries every two or three years. Right now I am in biotech and certain other high tech stocks. At other times I have been in automotive stocks. Then there was my metals phase.

If I ever came to accept the fact that I really don't hold stocks more than one or two years, and made a cost analysis, I might find out that it would have been cheaper to buy one or two nine month Calls on the stocks than to buy the stocks themselves. It certainly seems less risky. Look at an example:

When I buy 100 shares of IBM at $100 per share, I put up $10,000. My theoretical potential loss is $10,000. But if I buy a long term in-the-money Call, with little time value premium for, say, $5,000, I may achieve the same result at a lower theoretical risk and smaller out-of-pocket investment and the same upside potential.

Why don't I do it? Because no one buys stock thinking that it is going to go down. So few investors really consider the theoretical risk and cost because they are focused on the profit. In addition, it is hard to find long term in-the-money Calls that do not have a lot of time value premium in them, and therefore there may not be that many occasions where Calls can be used in place of stocks.

So that's why I put this discussion in the philosophical, or "principles" part of this book. This concept may not have a lot of practical value, but it is important to recognize the principle; namely that options control stock in such a way that the benefits to be achieved may be just as great or greater with the options, while the cost is much less. One major purpose of this book is to illustrate specific useful examples of this basic principle.

2. The next basic principle in this book is that the most likely way to profit from options is to sell options so as to capture time value premium. Selling options is called "writing." And so option writing is the key to profits as expounded in this book. This basic principle flows naturally from the underlying assumption that no one can accurately predict the market. By analogy, no one can accurately predict when they are going to die. We can judge, based on statistics, the average age we will achieve, depending on various groups in which we fit. As a white male living in Los Angeles smog, I think I have about 20 years to go, statistically. But I would not be willing to invest on that premise.

There are people that do invest according to that premise, however, and they do not really care about me individually, but they know that they can look at a lot of historical data and predict with pretty good accuracy how old several hundred thousand people like me will be at death. These people run insurance companies. And so the insurance company is willing to write a contract (an annuity) which makes money if I live less than 20 years. They will also write another contract (an insurance policy) that will make money if I live more than 20 years and lose money if I live less than 20 years. For either of these contracts I pay them a premium. If I pay the premium, the insurance company will take either assumption I elect.

That is how I view option writing, and that is the basic profit principle in this book. I sell you a contract to buy IBM stock at $100 a share. You pay me a $500 premium in exchange for my contract. I do it every month for 12 months, adjusting the price as IBM stock moves. I'm trying to be like an insurance company, and make money on the premium, not the movement of the stock.

Let's say that I know that historically IBM has not moved more than $5 per share in most months. (This is just an example. I have not really looked at the fluctuation of IBM month-by-month, and realize that it may be more than $5 per share). So, unless there is a fundamental change in the market or in IBM, most months I am going to get to keep the $500. Once in a while I am going to have to pay it back, and perhaps I will have to pay back more. That is exactly what happens to the life insurance company.

This leads to the next principle: Because we are operating on a principle which is based on statistical fluctuation, there can be wide variation from the norm.

So for 11 months I may keep your $500, and I will be $5,500 ahead. As long as I do not lose more than a reasonable portion of that $5,500 in the twelfth month, my strategy has worked. And, since I never know which month will be the "twelfth month," each month I try to hedge to prevent myself from losing more money than I expect to gain during a year with normal periods of fluctuation.

The implication to draw from this principle is that virtually all option writing should be hedged. In certain strategies the hedge is automatically present in the strategy, such as writing Puts to acquire stock, and in spreads. But this basic principle must be followed if one is to be philosophically consistent with the premises expressed here.

4. Finally, it seems to follow that writing Calls and Call spreads on an index is safer than writing on individual stocks, unless the investor has some other reason for owning the stock. For example, some investors are locked into a large stock portfolio which, for tax purposes, they do not want to liquidate. Some investors acquire stock as part of their employment, and are not legally permitted to sell it. And some investors make an investment decision to acquire certain stocks. But if one is investing according to the philosophy expressed above, and that person is writing options to acquire <u>time value premium,</u> writing the options on an index is safer because the diversity of stocks used in the index smoothes out the fluctua-

tions that can arise from significant market information about one company.

Undoubtedly, there are more underlying assumptions and more basic principles in this book than I have spelled out here. Part of the investment process is formulating your own assumptions and reaching your own basic principles from them.

PART III - Writing CALLS Against Instruments Other Than Stock

A. Writing CALLS against deep-in-the-money CALLS

Instead of using stock as an instrument to write CALLS against, to limit potential losses, you can buy other CALLS - which is much cheaper than buying the stock. When you sell a call and then buy one at a higher strike price to hedge, that's called a "spread." Spreads are discussed at length in Chapter IV. When you write such a spread, you have potential loss for the difference between strike prices. In other words, if you sell a 35 call and buy a 40 to hedge, you have a potential loss of 5 points, which on a typical position of 10 options gives you a potential liability of $5,000 less the premium income you take in on the sale part of the spread. But you can also buy an in-the-money call at a strike price below the current price of the stock to hedge your position. Such a call varies in price almost exactly the same as the stock, because the call price is virtually all intrinsic value without time value premium.

For example:

When Dupont (symbol DD) comes out with some good news, and the stock goes up to 44, I decide to sell the April 45 CALLS for 2 points. I sell 10 CALLS, for a gross premium received of $2,000. I could hedge by buying 1,000 shares of Dupont for $44,000. This would amount to a "buy-write" where I buy the stock at 44 and sell the 45 calls. Or I could create a spread by buying the 50 calls.

Alternatively, I can <u>buy</u> 10 CALLS of the <u>July</u> 40's for, say 5 points, paying $5,000 but giving me a right to buy the stock I don't have for $40,000. I am "out of pocket" $3,000 right away. But, of course, that's less than the $42,000 I would have to come up with if I bought the stock.

If the stock stays at 44 until the third Friday of April, on that date the April calls expire worthless, allowing me to keep the $2,000 in April premiums. Then I sell the 40 calls that I bought to hedge. I would expect to receive at least $4,500 ($4,000 for intrinsic value, and $500 for time value for the reduced period between April and July from the original date when I bought the option—a decline of 50% of the time value premium). So I lose $500 on the July Calls, as if I had paid an insurance premium, but I make $2,000 on the April Calls, for a net profit of $1,500.

Not bad for picking a stock that DIDN'T go up.

If the stock does go up, I will lose $1,000 on the April Calls for each point it goes up over $45, but make $1,000 on the July Calls for each point. So I'm hedged on the upside, and even have another $1,000 in profit to pick up between $44 and $45.

So long as the stock price stays above the long call strike price, here $40, a decline in the stock price costs me the same as if I had bought the stock, with one difference: part of the time value premium I paid (in my example 1/2 point, or $500) will be lost. That amount may or may not be equal to the value of the use of the money saved by not buying the stock. If the stock falls below $40, I am no longer hedged. In this case I should buy back the 40 Calls and rewrite the 35's. See the discussion of "rolling strategies" in Chapter IV.

B. Warrants

Not as many warrants are issued today as was the case in the past. The junk bond market replaced the warrants market as a marketing device to induce investment. With the decline of the junk bond market, warrants may once again become popular. Meanwhile, there still are a number of warrants outstanding, from previous issues, which are actively traded. The warrant analysis requires a determination of whether the strike price is in-the-money or out-of-the-money. The volatility of the stock price should be compared to the volatility of the warrant price to determine the appropriate ratio for writing a CALL. Of course, not all warrants are issued on optionable stock, and therefore one must also make sure that the stock is optionable and that there is sufficient liquidity in the options on the stock to be able to sell CALLS with enough premium to make the strategy worthwhile.

An example of writing CALLS against warrants is the XXX CORP 5/15/06 warrant. This hypothetical warrant might permit purchase of a share of XXX stock at $15. The stock might be currently traded at $21. The price of the warrant might be $10. This represents a $4 premium over the $6 intrinsic value of the warrant. However, XXX August 25 CALL options may be priced at $2.25. The possibility exists of buying the warrants and selling the CALLS. The cost of the warrants would be less than half the cost of the stock. It might be possible to write CALLS several times against the warrants before they expire.

C. Convertible Bonds

Convertible bonds are bonds which have a "kicker" that gives the bond holder the right to exchange the bonds for stock in the company under certain conditions. This "kicker" is very much like an option or a warrant. The nice thing about convertible bonds is that the investment you make pays interest while you are waiting to see if your option becomes valuable. The bad part of convertible bonds is that they usually pay less interest than you could get somewhere else because they have the "kicker" attached to them.

Where the bonds are convertible into optionable stock, some investors mentally cull out the option feature of the bond, treat it like an option, and write other options on the underlying stock in conjunction with the option feature of the convertible bond.

For example, K-Mart 6% July 1999 bonds were convertible to 28.17 shares. That is, each $1,000 face value of bonds could be converted to 28.17 shares of common stock. If the common stock was selling for $30 per share, the conversion value of the bonds would be $845.10. The price of the bond might be $900. This would make the yield 6.6%. In most cases the yield on a convertible bond is greater than the dividend on the stock. The bond can be used to cover the risk of writing options on the stock in place of the stock, which has a poorer yield than the bond. Note that the conversion ratio, in this case 28.17, must be considered in determining how many options can be sold. For example, 25 bonds ($25,000 face and $22,500 cost) would be convertible in 25 times 28.17 or 704.25 shares, and could cover writing 7 options on the stock.

It is not part of the philosophy espoused in this book to write options in conjunction with convertible bonds, except insofar as the bonds are treated as a bond portfolio. This is discussed in the section on Hedging Against

Interest Rate Fluctuations. Convertible bonds are really a business unto themselves, and to evaluate the underlying option writing potential requires a lot of investigation into the underlying terms of the bond indenture, as well as the company itself. The purchase of the bonds requires a large capital investment, and therefore when writing calls for the purpose of capturing time value premiums, the underlying stock is generally more suitable than the convertible bond.

As shown in the above example, however, if one is inclined to own convertible bonds anyway, one can use them as a vehicle for capturing CALL premiums, while being hedged by the convertible feature of the bonds. The investor should make a careful analysis of the relationship between fluctuation in the stock and the value of the bond to determine the appropriate ratio of CALLS to write against each bond and still remain reasonably hedged. This may be difficult to do with convertible bonds because of the interplay between interest rates and underlying stock price on the value of the bonds.

D. Hedging Against Interest Rate Fluctuations

This strategy is of particular interest to investors with a bond portfolio. The value of bonds fluctuates inversely to interest rates. For example, when a key interest rate is 8%, bond issues which pay 8% will sell at par ($1,000 per bond). If that key rate goes up to 9 %, that bond becomes less valuable. A new investor could buy a bond like the one you bought, for par, and get a 9% return. So he is not going to pay you par for your bond. He will probably only pay you just under $900 for your bond. Then when he gets his $80 return on your bond, he has gotten approximately the same 9% return which he could get somewhere else, since 9% of $900 is $81.

So now that interest rates are at 9%, your bond has dropped from $1,000 value to $900 value. Of course, if interest rates go down to 7%, your bond is more valuable, because now the investor cannot go out and buy a bond that pays 8% for a $1,000 investment.

Whenever the investor with a bond portfolio is primarily interested in conservation of invested capital, with a reasonable rate of return which, at a minimum, will keep up with the rate of inflation, option writing is the ideal situation for him.

To prevent a decrease in the portfolio, one can buy or write options on an interest index so that if interest rates decline, and the bond portfolio goes up in value, the investor has given up some of that increase by paying out option premiums. Conversely, if interest rates go up, and the value of the bond portfolio declines, the option investor makes a profit on the options, which can be geared to approximate the loss on the bonds.

Banks often follow this strategy to protect their underlying bond investment portfolio. The bank is not buying the bonds to profit from capital appreciation, but to maintain adequate capital to meet federal regulations. To protect against this capital declining, and thereby falling below the federal regulations, smart banks protect their bank portfolios with options. There are specialists who do nothing but handle this kind of transaction on behalf of banks.

One way to hedge the bond portfolio is to buy options on the interest index. We can also sell interest rate spreads to take in time value premium. Even if you don't have a bond portfolio, you can do that, but if you have a bond portfolio, it is a particularly good way of capturing time value premium and hedge your bond portfolio at the same time. A discussion of the interest index is beyond the scope of this book, since I promised not to make it encyclopedic. Suffice to say that there are two main indexes, one that follows government bond index rates, and one that follows municipal bond index rates. Sometimes it is hard to write options on the municipal bond index, because there is not always much activity, and it sometimes lacks buyers and sellers. The regular interest index has a lot of activity on it, and it is a very highly leveraged market with a lot of speculation. It is very easy to lose a lot of money on it very quickly. It is particularly complicated because the numbers are inverted - that is, when interest rates go up, the index numbers go down and vice versa. It is also complicated because the numbers do not mean what they say, and are not expressed in decimals. So you have to learn a whole new language, and turn your mind upside down.

Writing options on an interest index is not for the faint of heart, but for those who want to study it a little more I present the following actual example of a typical interest rate spread:

On May 4, 1991 Treasury Bond Futures were quoted:

May 90 0-53   May 92 0-13

This means that a May 90 Treasury Bond Future was priced at 53/64 or $828.10 per contract. The May 92's were 13/64 or $203.10 per contract.

The following spread was put on:

Sold 10 May 90's $8,281 credit

Bought 10 May 92's   (2,031) cost

Gross credit $6,250

less: $350 per position commission (700)

NET PROCEEDS $5,550

The hope was that interest rates would go up and the value of the short contracts would decrease. If interest rates increased so that the price was below $90 per hundred (in $100,000 increments) the futures would expire worthless and the net proceeds could be kept.

However, interest rates declined and the price of the contracts increased. The price of the May 90's at the close of the contracts was 1-36 or 1 and 36/64ths. The May 92's expired worthless.

The cost of buying back the 10 May 90 Treasury Bond contracts was $15,625 plus $350 commission or $15,975.00.

The final result of this spread was a loss of $15,975 less the initial net proceeds of $5,550 - a $10,425 loss. As I said, writing options on an interest index is not for the faint of heart.

There are several interest indexes, which are tied to various instruments. Some even have options available, which reduce the cost of using them as hedges. But be careful: some have very little liquidity, so the pricing spread can be unpredictable. So check the sales volume before committing to use a particular index.

E. Long Term Options-LEAPS

The principles of selling long term options should be exactly the same as selling traditional options, and the question to be investigated is whether the ratio of time value premium to historical stock volatility is at least as much as with traditional options. The amount of time value premium for the remaining life of the option is a key factor in the potential profitability of a writing strategy. This figure is often influenced by demand. As long term options become more popular, I would expect to see the time value premium on options on volatile stocks expand.

The following is an example of a trade which could be made today with long term options:

On October 26, 2004, the following long term CALL options on IBM were available:

IBM   INTL BUSINESS MACHINES CORP   NYSE
Price: 89.000 Chg: 0.570 %Chg: 0.64% Volume: 7,337,300   Date/Time: 10/26/2004 16:01:00
Option Quote

WCXAJ	CALL JAN 2006 @ 50.000	50	39.400	N/A	N/A	N/A	0	10/25/2004
WCXAK	CALL JAN 2006 @ 55.000	55	34.700	N/A	N/A	N/A	0	10/25/2004
WCXAL	CALL JAN 2006 @ 60.000	60	30.700	0.500	30.400	30.800	5	10/26/2004 14:33:00
WCXAM	CALL JAN 2006 @ 65.000	65	25.600	N/A	N/A	N/A	0	10/25/2004
WIBAN	CALL JAN 2006 @ 70.000	70	21.450	-0.150	21.500	21.900	0	10/25/2004 00:00:00
WIBAO	CALL JAN 2006 @ 75.000	75	17.700	1.900	17.400	17.800	11	10/26/2004 13:51:00
WIBAP	CALL JAN 2006 @ 80.000	80	13.350	N/A	N/A	N/A	0	10/25/2004
WIBAQ	CALL JAN 2006 @ 85.000	85	10.000	N/A	N/A	N/A	0	10/25/2004
WIBAR	CALL JAN 2006 @ 90.000	90	7.400	0.700	7.300	7.500	7	10/26/2004 12:28:00
WIBAS	CALL JAN 2006 @ 95.000	95	4.900	0.000	4.900	5.100	56	10/26/2004 15:41:00
WIBAT	CALL JAN 2006 @ 100.000	100	3.300	0.100	3.200	3.400	101	10/26/2004 12:13:00
WIBAA	CALL JAN 2006 @ 105.000	105	2.050	0.150	2.000	2.100	14	10/26/2004 12:19:00
WIBAB	CALL JAN 2006 @ 110.000	110	1.300	0.150	1.150	1.300	141	10/26/2004 15:41:00
WIBAD	CALL JAN 2006 @ 120.000	120	0.400	0.000	0.400	0.500	30	10/26/2004 12:24:00
WIBAF	CALL JAN 2006 @ 130.000	130	0.150	N/A	N/A	N/A	0	10/25/2004
WIBAH	CALL JAN 2006 @ 140.000	140	0.100	N/A	N/A	N/A	0	10/25/2004
WIBAJ	CALL JAN 2006 @ 150.000	150	0.050	N/A	N/A	N/A	0	10/25/2004
WIBAL	CALL JAN 2006 @ 160.000	160	0.050	N/A	N/A	N/A	0	10/25/2004

Option Quote Lookup

The Jan 2006 IBM 100 CALLS were trading at approximately $3.30 (I've taken the mean between bid and ask). If IBM were to remain below $100 these would expire worthless. It would be possible to buy a January 2006 IBM 100 Call for $330 and use this to cover writing of several calls during 2005. The April 95's of 2005's are bid $1.75. In April perhaps I can sell some July's for another $1.75 and then write one more time in October or November. If so, and if the premiums are about the same (unlikely, but OK as an example) I might take in over $500 in premium, hedged at a cost of $330, for a profit of $170. The cost of the long term option to cover these writes would be only $330 rather than $8,900 to buy 100 shares of the stock. Of course, the option would not pay a dividend. If IBM fell to $70 per share the loss on shares purchased at $89 would be $1,900, while the loss on the January option would be the $330 that the option cost, less the premium income.

As a practical matter I would not keep the long position until it expires. As discussed below, the best way to deal with a long position used to hedge is to sell it before the steep part of the decline curve and rewrite a position further out until all positions are closed out. More on this later.

F. Gold

Gold and investments tied to gold are often used for hedging purposes. Many economists and investors have various theories about how gold prices will react in times of inflation, deflation, rising economies and falling economies, as well as during periods when the dollar is falling or rising. Some investors write options on gold futures as a way of investing in gold (or shorting it) with higher leverage. As with other precious metals, gold futures are traded on the commodities market.

Since the prices of stocks in companies that produce gold typically follow the price of gold itself, and the price of companies that use a lot of gold are adversely impacted by increases in gold prices, some investors buy gold futures and then write puts or calls on securities tied to gold prices, directly or indirectly.

If you find yourself long gold or gold stocks that don't trade options, you should consider investigating this opportunity, either by selling options on appropriate stocks, or options in the gold market itself.

G. Private Options and Collars

While the discussions in this book center on publicly traded options, there are a number of private options written each year. Many institutions, primarily banks, provide a service to clients by arranging to buy or sell options from the client on stock which is either not publicly traded, or which is publicly traded but not optionable on any market.

Because of the variety of arrangements that are available, it is beyond the scope of this book to detail them. In addition, the complex strategies employed by the banks and other institutions to hedge such transactions and make them possible is a study in itself. But there is one transaction which is common enough to warrant an explanation here, and it is called the "collar." The collar arises in the public market also, but it is a favorite transaction in private options for the reasons explained below.

Investors are often "stuck" with large stock positions which, for one reason or another, they do not wish to sell. Three common example are (1) where the investor has a very low basis in the stock and doesn't want to pay the capital gain tax on sale, (2) where the stock is in a family business, and the investor doesn't want to disturb the market by selling a large block, and (3) where the stock is restricted, for example under the Securities and Exchange ("S.E.C.") rules, and cannot be legally sold for some period of time.

By way of illustration, let us consider the third example. Mr. Schmidt takes his company public, and retains $10 million worth of stock after the public offering. The stock is restricted and cannot be sold for two years. Mr. Schmidt fears that interest rates will move up, and his holdings will decline very substantially before he can legally begin to liquidate the stock.

In this situation, after consulting his securities attorney, Mr. Schmidt may go to a bank that performs private option services, and put a collar on his position. The most common collar would be the purchase of a Put and the simultaneous sale of a Call, where the premiums are approximately equal. For example, if Mr. Schmidt's stock is trading at $20 per share, the bank might sell him a put with a strike price of $15 per share, and buy a call from him with a strike price of $23 per share, with no cash changing hands. Typically the bank does this either because it can resell its positions and make a small premium on the sale, or because it can buy and sell offsetting options on the market (since it is not subject to the legal restriction) at a slightly less net cost.

Why does Mr. Schmidt do this? By buying the puts at a $15 strike price, he is protected against a decline of more than 25% in the stock price. In exchange for this protection, he is giving up any increase in the stock above $23 per share. He is willing to give up this "upside" since he feels that he has a large enough holding, and for the insurance that the holding will not decline below $7.5 million.

The variety of private options which can be tailored for individual needs is amazing, and several banks have experts available to construct such transactions for wealthy stockholders. These institutions also provide such services as purchasing restricted stock (at a discount, usually ranging from 5-15%) under the "off-shore" exemption to the S.E.C. rules.

PART IV - Combinations and Complex Strategies for Conservative Investors

First let me assure you that I am not going to discuss in this text all of the really fancy strategies used in the options market. Those of you active in the market have certainly heard of strips and straps, strangles and reverse repo hedging. I am not doing that here, although I will mention the straddle in passing. I am only going to discuss a few of the most commonly used option strategies. There are enough of those to keep us very busy and there are not that many people who understand even those few that we discuss here. The common threads of these strategies are: (1) each has a defined risk; and, (2) in each, we expect to profit by capturing time value premium from the sale of an option.

A. Spreads

Spreads are pretty complicated because there are so many different kinds. Again, the vocabulary of spreads is what makes it difficult for most people to think about them. I am not sure that it is necessary to know the vocabulary of spreads to make money from doing them. But if you make money from doing them and want to talk about them to your friends, here goes.

A basic concept of the spread is that there are two options which have some relationship. The relationship usually is that both positions are on the same stock, and are designed to act together in some way that accomplishes a goal. For the moment, let's take the simple cases and define spreads as two options on the same security. With this starting point, spreads can be classified in a number of ways:

Calendar Spreads. The calendar spread is a combination of two options with the <u>same strike price</u> and a <u>different expiration date</u>. In other words, the two parts of the spread consist of options that expire on different calendar dates. An example of the calendar spread is the sale of a Ford 35 CALL expiring in January and the purchase of a Ford 40 CALL expiring in April. (See Figure IV-1.)

One main reason for entering into a calendar spread is to take advantage of the time value decline line. Since an option loses its entire time value premium by expiration date, there is some amount of time value premium that it loses on each trading day between the day the buyer sells it and the date it expires. In other words, if you buy for $2 an out-of-the-money option ten trading days before it

FIGURE IV-1 Calendar Spread (Out-of-the-Money)

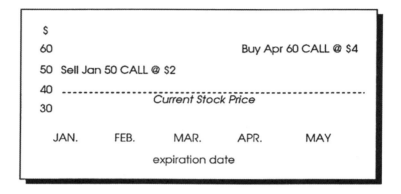

If you collect a $2 premium on the sale and pay out a $4 premium on the purchase, this is a "debit spread," where you have a $2 debit at the opening. If the stock price stays below $50 when the January option expires you will be able to close out the April option and keep the premium collected on the January option. The risk of loss is small, because (1) there is a large "window" (10 points), and (2) if the stock price goes beyond $50, the April position value will increase so the sale of it will cover some of the loss of the January position.

Premiums this high would only be available in a stock viewed by the Market as quite volatile.

expires and it stays out-of-the-money, it will lose $2 of value in the ten remaining trading days. But it will probably not lose 20 cents on each of those ten days. Time value changes depending partly on the price of the stock, that is, how far out-of-the-money it stays, and there is also a tendency for the value to depreciate more quickly the closer it is to the expiration date. Generally speaking, a lot of the time value premium seems to disappear during the last 30 days of an option's life, and the decline in value seems to accelerate quickly during the last two or three weeks of its life. See Figure I-6.

For this reason, some investors seeking to capture time value premium write calendar spreads by selling a short term position such that the premium expires quickly, and buying a longer term position to hedge, which has not lost all of it's time value premium if closed out when the earlier position expires.

Price Spreads. A price spread is where the <u>expiration date of both positions is the same</u>, but <u>the strike price is different</u>. For example: When Ford is at $35, I sell a Ford 40 CALL and buy a Ford 45 CALL, both expiring in 30 days. The purpose of such a spread is to capture the time-value premium of the 40 CALL, while limiting the risk to five points (between $40 and $45). We will examine such reasoning when we talk about the purposes for spreads below.

Bull and Bear Spreads. Another way to characterize spreads is as "bull spreads" and "bear spreads." The bull spread is a spread in which the investor makes a profit if the underlying stock or index goes up; the bear spread is a spread in which the investor will lose money if the underlying stock or index goes up and make money if the underlying stock or index goes down. It is convenient to think about spreads in terms of bull or bear, just to check your hypothesis in investing.

Here is an example of a common bull spread (see Figure IV-2):

With ZZZ at $99, I sell 10 of the 100 PUTS and buy 10 of the 90 PUTS, to hedge, for a net credit of $6,000. If ZZZ goes up over 100 (and stays there until expiration,) I make $6,000. My risk of loss was $9,000 less $6,000, or $3,000. The maximum loss arises if ZZZ goes to or below 90, since I lose $1,000 for each point below 99, down to the hedge at 90. So my profit arises from a bull market, at least as to ZZZ.

Here is an example of a bear spread (see Figure IV-3):

With YYY at $101, I sell one 100 CALL and buy one 105 CALL, for a net credit of $200. This is a bear spread because it profits if the stock goes down, but loses if the stock goes up. The worst case is a rise over $105, which will result in a net loss of $300, $500 less the $200 premium.

FIGURE IV-2 Bull Spread.

Initial Position	At Expiration
$	$
100 ---- Sell $100 PUT for $10	100 Maximum profit $6
99 ---- $99 stock price	99 When stock is above $100
98	98
97	97
96	96 } Profit range
95	95 } When stock is above $94
94	94
93	93 }
92	92 } Loss range
91	91 When stock is under $94
90 ---- Buy $90 PUT for $4	90
89	89 Maximum loss $4
	When stock is below $90

This is a _Bull Spread_ because (1) you are short and long the same security at a different price, creating a spread, and (2) it's "bullish" because you profit when the security goes _up_ and lose when it goes _down_.

I believe that most CALL spreads written are bear spreads.

Credit and Debit Spreads. A credit spread is one where the option sold creates more premium than the option bought when the position is put on. (See Figure IV-4). For example, most price spreads are credit spreads, because you sell the option at the closer strike price - therefore more valuable - and buy the cheaper option at the further strike price.

A debit spread is where you pay out money when the spread is placed. A calendar spread is sometimes a debit spread, where you buy an expensive option with more time left on it that the one you sell.

Like price spreads and calendar spreads, these terms are only helpful for purposes of discussing spreads; none of these terms helps in understanding the reason behind the decision to make investment in the spread. For that reason, I prefer to classify spreads in two categories: (1) spreads to reduce the cost of a primary position, and (2) spreads to hedge a position. Let's take a look at an example of each.

Spreads to reduce the cost of a primary position. Let's assume that VVV stock is at $45. I plan to buy ten CALLS of the VVV 50's expiring in approximately 90 days. I do this because I think that VVV will go up 10 to 20% in the next 90 days, that is, up to the range of $50 to

FIGURE IV-3 Bear Spread.

In this example, the 100 CALL is sold and the 105 CALL bought for a net credit of $2 per option. The maximum loss per option is $300 if the stock goes above $105 ($500 minus the $200 premium received). If the stock declines in value below $100 the profit is $200 for each option contract. Some additional profit might be made by selling the long 105 position before expiration.

This is a "bear" spread because you make money if the stock goes down.

FIGURE IV-4 An Out-of-the-Money PUT (Credit) Spread.

If stock stays above 40 until expiration, seller keeps a $100 premium ($100 per put because 1 put equates to 100 shares).

If stock goes below 40, the buyer of the 40 PUT will "put" the stock to seller, forcing seller to buy 100 shares at $40, no matter how low the stock falls. The seller can either take delivery of the stock, buy back the option before expiration, or buy the stock on the market to deliver to the buyer. (Note that the "seller" of the option becomes the equivalent of a "buyer" of the stock, if "put").

Between 30–40, seller is at risk up to $900 (10 points times 100 shares less $100 premium received).

Below 30 the seller profits $100 on the 30 PUT for each additional $100 of loss on the 40 PUT.

$54. The CALLS cost $2, so for ten CALLS (controlling 1,000 shares) I pay $2,000. I expect to make as much as $2,000 (doubling my money) if my presumption is right and VVV goes up to $54. In other words, if VVV goes up to $54, the 50 CALLS I bought will be $4 in-the-money and worth $4,000 at expiration, so I take in $4,000 and will have paid out $2,000. In order to reduce my cost, however, and increase my potential percentage return, at the same time, I sell 10 VVV 55 CALLS. For this sale I receive 50 cents, or $500 for ten CALLS. Now I am long the VVV 50's, and short the VVV 55's, a sort of bull price spread. My cost is now only $1,500, or 25% less than if I only bought the VVV 50's. I have a risk of loss $1,500, which is my out-of-pocket cost. My maximum gain is limited to $3,500 ($5,000 less the $1,500 cost) by the 55 CALLS sold because if VVV goes over $55 the 55 CALL will lose the same amount as any further profit from the 50 CALLS. (See Figure IV-5.)

Spreads to hedge a position. Suppose that telephone stock is at $45. I sell the 50 CALLS 30 days out. I do this because I do not expect telephone to go up 5 points during the next 30 days. Nevertheless, I am uncomfortable about it. If telephone becomes a takeover candidate, the stock might go to $70 pr $80. To protect, or hedge my position, I buy the 55 CALLS with the same expiration date. Assuming I have bought and sold ten of each, my maximum loss is now $5,000 less the net premium received on the spread. Until expiration day, if telephone stays between $45 and $50, I get to keep the

FIGURE IV-5 Spread to Reduce the Cost of a Primary Position (Unusual)

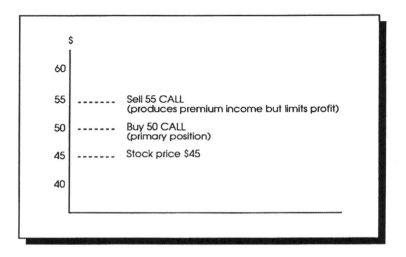

entire net premium. Between $50 and $55 I will lose $1,000 per point, less the net premium I received. Over $55 my long 55 CALL will gain intrinsic value the same amount that my short 50 CALL loses for each point that the stock goes up. I have limited my risk to a fixed dollar maximum. This is one of the key factors in conservative option investing.

B. Boxes

Now that you are familiar with spreads, it is time to extend that concept to the "box." A box is a combination of two spreads, one on each side of the current price of the underlying stock or index. (See Figure IV-6.)

Let us look at an example:

With the OEX at $300, I put on a CALL spread by selling a 320 CALL (short) and buying a 330 CALL (long). Then I put on a PUT spread where I sell A 280 PUT and buy a 270 PUT. On the CALL spread I might have received $2,000 on the 320 and paid $1,000 for buying the 270, for a net credit of $1,000. Perhaps the prices on the put side are the same, although typically puts have higher premiums than calls. On a typical transaction of ten of each position, I should therefore get a credit of at least $4,000, less $2,000 paid out, for a net credit of $2,000. Let us look at the effect of putting on this box.

Assume that these are all 30 day positions. If the OEX

FIGURE IV-6 The Box Spread.

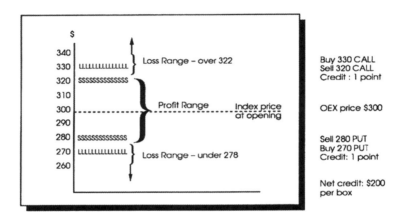

At expiration (except in cases of premature assignment):

Between 280 and 320 seller keeps the premium.
Over 322 and under 278 seller loses $100 per point.

The maximum profit is $200 and the maximum loss is $800 ($1,000–$200) on the entire position.

While twice as much premium is collected compared to a single spread, the risk of any loss occurring has also doubled. The potential amount of loss is slightly mitigated because at expiration there can only be a loss on one of the spreads.

In this illustration, the line of "L's" stands for "Long", and line of "S's" stands for "short".

stays between the range of $280 and $320 during the 30 days, I keep the $2,000 in net premium. All of the positions, including the long positions, will expire worthless. In other words, I will have made a profit of $4,000 on the short positions, and lost $2,000 on the long positions. If the OEX goes outside of my short positions in either direction, I will lose $1,000 per point below my short Call, up to my long position—-10 points away. So my risk of loss is $10,000 less the $2,000 I received, or $8,000.

One way to look at this as investor is to make an analysis of the OEX. Will it vary 30 points in either direction during a 30 day period more than 20% of the time? If so, statistically I will lose money by repeated writing of this position. If it will not vary more than 20 points in a typical 30 day period more than 20% of the time, I will make money. In other words, taking a $2,000 profit in an investment with a $10,000 loss potential is OK if you will make the $2,000 more than 5 times as often as you lose the $10,000. Sophisticated option writers actually do historical analysis like this, but the formulas are much more complicated than this paragraph suggests.

The box exposes you to greater risk than the simple spread (contrary to what many brokers will tell you). With the box, you have twice the chance to lose in case of unexpected volatility. But because the stock (or index) can only end up either up or down - not both - the box is safer than writing two unrelated spreads and is therefore appropriate, in my opinion, for the investor who writes spreads repeatedly.

C. The In-And-Out Strategy

As a result of writing uncovered PUTS on selected stocks, investors are sometimes put the stock and thereby become the proud owners of that stock. This has led to a strategy I call "in-and-out," in which the investor keeps writing PUTS until put the stock, then writes CALLS until the stock is called away. The process is repeated until the stock is at a price (either through price change or change of the investor's perception of the company) at which there is insufficient premium in the PUT, at a desirable strike price, to make the strategy profitable.

Here is an example:

Having investigated MMM stock, I become convinced that it has an intrinsic value of $60 which will someday be realized. The stock now sells for $53. At $50 I decide it is a bargain. On February 10 I sell 10 PUTS of the March 50's, for 2 points, receiving $2,000 in premium.

MMM now drops to $48 and in March I am put 1,000 shares.

I now sell the April 50 CALLS and collect $1500 in premium. At this point I own 1,000 shares for which I paid $50,000 and have collected $3,500 in premium, so my net cost is approximately $48 after transaction costs.

If the stock goes to $50 and is called away from me, I

let it go, and may start the process over with a new PUT position.

If the stock continues to decline, I continue to write CALLS against it. If I believe the decline is serious, I may write the 45 CALL, collecting some intrinsic value as a hedge against the continued decline in the stock price, particularly if there is no significant premium in the 50 CALL, as the stock price moves down.

If the stock goes below $45. I write the 45 CALLS planning to roll up to the 50's when the stock rebounds.

If the stock stays below $45 and I become convinced that it will not recover in the near future, I may hold the stock or I may sell it, to free up capital and take a $5,000+ loss in the stock, which will be partially or fully made up in the premium income. Note: With volatile stocks the drop can be substantially more than the premium income. Nevertheless, I consider this a reasonably conservative strategy, because it seems to me to be significantly safer in terms of capital protection than buying stock at the market and holding it for long-term appreciation. Here you have the protection of the first premium, and the potential for continued premium income.

D. Straddles and Rolling-Rewrite Strategies

Straddles are another way to benefit from volatility or

lack of volatility, depending on whether you buy or sell them. To buy a traditional straddle the investor buys an option with a strike price on each side of the market, thereby benefiting from a change in price over a certain percentage during the life of the option. (See Figure IV-7.)

For example:

With the OEX at $300, I buy 10 CALLS of the 310's and I buy 10 PUTS of the 290's. I pay $4,000 in premium. I profit if the market goes over $314 or under $286. Just before the first war in Iraq, some brokers were recommending the purchase of an OEX 290 PUT, coupled with the sale of the 280 PUT to reduce the cost, on the theory that war would cause the market to plummet. As we know, at the outset of the war the market jumped over 130 points on the Dow Jones Industrial Average in two days. Even without hindsight the straddle was a better selection of investment.

If both options are reversed (the PUT above the market and the CALL below), the options are in-the-money and the risk is point-for-point with the market. This is sometimes called a strangle.

A somewhat popular strategy is to write a straddle really a straddle/strangle) on the OEX at the money, hedging the downside risk (but usually not the upside) against catastrophe and rewriting on a rolling-rewrite basis (once a week, or once a month). At least one major

FIGURE IV-7 Straddle.

BUYER'S VIEWPOINT

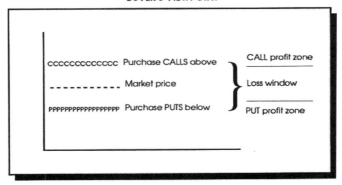

The buyer expects the market to be volatile, and pass beyond the option strike prices during the life of the options.

The profit window for the seller is wider than for the buyer because the buyer pays the Time Value Premium and the seller receives it. The seller is at high risk.

SELLER'S VIEWPOINT

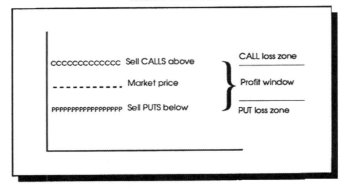

NYSE brokerage firm currently supports several of its brokers in providing this service to investors with at least $1 million to invest in the market. It is contended that statistically the market will not deviate as much as the premiums will support if this strategy is followed. Historically this may well be true, but there are two risks to this kind of investment which you should always factor in:

RISK #1. To maintain the kind of discipline required for any rolling strategy requires a substantially full-time market watch. It is not for the person who takes an occasional vacation. Therefore, this kind of strategy is best left to professionals to handle.

RISK #2. Some would-be gamblers try to beat Las Vegas by doubling-up their bet each time they lose. This usually works for awhile, but eventually a streak of bad luck will cause the bet to be too high - either for the bettor or for the house limit and at that point the bettor is broke.

This can also happen in these rolling strategies. At some point a major or sustained rise or drop will occur and even with discipline in closing out losses, your capital can be depleted to the point where you can no longer continue the strategy.

For there reasons I am wary of these rolling strategies, even when professionally handled and would only invest in them if my capital is pooled with others, the load from such a pool is not excessive and the pool keeps ample reserves to continue investing in the face of a significant loss.

E. Open Combinations
[NOT Really Conservative]

Many option writers (but vastly fewer now than before the October 1987 crash!) sell an out-of-the-money CALL and an out-of-the-money PUT on stocks and the OEX. (See Figure IV-8.) Properly structured such a strategy makes sense, although it is not a conservative investment.

For example: suppose I consider HHH, currently at $105, a bargain at $100, and I would be willing to own 100 shares at that price. In addition to selling a 100 PUT, I also sell a 110 CALL. I take in $2 on each side, for $4 net. If HHH goes down to $100 or below, I own it at a net cost of $96 per share. If is appears to be going over $114 I take a small loss (at, say, $112) and roll up the combination to a 105 PUT and a 120 CALL. If I can carefully watch the stock, and it does not run up too fast, this can be a successful strategy on specially selected stocks with adequate premiums. (See Figure IV-9.) But the conservative investor hedges the short CALL with a long CALL - in this case, by buying the 120 or 125 at the outset. (See Figure IV-10.)

The same strategy can be followed on the OEX, but

FIGURE IV-8 The "Unhedged" Combination:
A Misunderstood, High Risk Strategy.

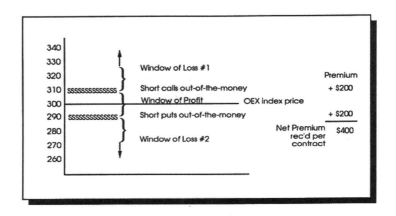

Some investors — and brokers! — are confused by this strategy. They think that because a short position is written on both sides, they are hedged. In fact, by writing on both sides the risk of loss has been doubled, and the only hedge is the extra $200 of premium. That's not much hedge for a potential loss of several thousand dollars!

Note the two large windows of loss.

here the conservative investor always hedges the down-side with a long position and keeps well out-of-the-money on the CALL side.

Hedging on the upside is thought by some to be less necessary because of two factors:

(1) The potential to partially hedge against a steep increase by maintaining a broad portfolio; and

(2) Historically, major declines have been more precipitous and created more disruption in pricing, than major increases.

These kinds of open combination can be appropriate for very aggressive option investors who carefully control the amount of risk and are consistently in touch with the market.

F. Three Way "Buy-Write" Combinations

Some very conservative investors add protection to the buy-write strategy. In the buy-write, the investor buys stock and writes out-of-the-money CALLS against it (as described in Part 2-C). The major risk of loss is that the stock price will fall more than the CALL premium. To pro-tect against that, in some cases it makes sense to buy an out-of-the-money PUT, to hedge against a decline in the stock price (See Figure IV-10.) This only makes good sense when the net CALL premium is greater than the net PUT premium.

FIGURE IV-9 The "PUT and CALL Spread" Combination

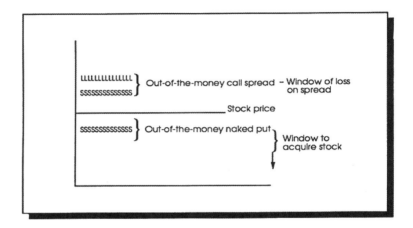

This combination is for the bearish investor who is willing to acquire the stock if it drops, at a price reduced by both a PUT premium and a premium from a CALL spread. The investor is multi-hedged: Hedged against loss on the CALL spread with the PUT premium, and hedged against being put the stock by both premiums.

G. Pricing Issues in Writing Spreads

One of the most important decisions to be made by the investor who is writing options spreads for premium income is "is it worth it?" In other words, is the amount of premium worth the risk of loss? Some sophisticated investors use a computer model for this analysis. Such a model uses investor-entered parameters to evaluate the risk and likely extent of loss, and compares the ratio of maximum loss to premium received.

Most of us have to just use a rule of thumb. In writing spreads on an index, my rule of thumb is that I expect that my maximum likely loss will not be more than twice the premium I take in. Then I try to write the spread sufficiently far out of the money such that I believe there is not more than a two-to-one likelihood of the worst case occurring.

For example, some time ago the Hong Kong index was attracting attention. It stood at approximately 258.The investor could sell 10 (out of the money) calls, December 270's, and buy 10 calls, December 280's, for a credit of $4,250—call it $4,000 after commissions. The underlying assumption is that that market will not go up more than 16 points by the December expiration date (12 points to 270 plus the 4 points of premium received).

At first blush this would not seem to meet the suggested rule of thumb, since there is a 10 point spread, and thus a potential loss of $10,000, and a $4,000 net premium, the ratio is 40%, not 50%.

But the spread writer must look at the potential loss somewhat differently: if the index goes up, the short position (here, the 270) will increase in value, creating a prospective loss. At the same time, the long position (here, the 280) will increase in value, creating a prospective profit. This will be true for most of the life of the spread, except for the last 2-3 weeks when the time value will wane.

This means that for most of the life of the spread, if the worst case comes true and the index goes to 280 or higher, creating the maximum possible loss on the short position, there will nevertheless be some gain on the long position. From experience one can estimate that to be, perhaps, one point (a lot depends on when this sharp rise occurs in the life cycle of the spread). So, the real maximum LIKELY loss is more like $9,000 or so, not $10,000, and the ratio of premium to likely loss is better than 50%—a good trade (if you are bearish on the Hong Kong market).

FIGURE IV-10 The "Three-way" Combination.

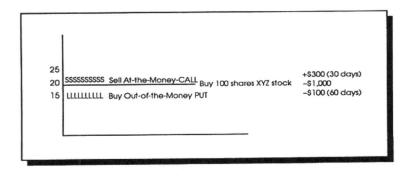

This investor is trying to capture a high-risk (and therefore high premium) CALL premium, hedged on the upside with the stock and on the downside with the long PUT.

If the stock goes up in the next 30 days, it will be called away at cost, and the investor will sell the PUT and keep the net premium on the CALL, less the loss on the PUT (decline in value over 30 days of its 60 day life).

If the stock goes down, the PUT value will increase, offsetting some of that loss.

The main problem with this strategy is that commissions usually eat up the potential profits.

PART V - Mitigating Strategies and Taking Profits and Losses

As soon as you put on your positions, a moment later they may change dramatically. When this happens, you are faced with various decisions, which are typically as follows:

1. Do nothing;

2. Take a profit and terminate further risk;

3. Accept a loss or allow a losing position to continue to escalate;

4. Hedge a winning or losing position;

5. Start over with a new position;

6. Increase or decrease a position.

I believe that it is in this decision making process that

most option writers lose money. They typically lose by deviating from their basic premise (capturing premium) and because of an unwillingness to accept loss.

A. Understanding The Psychology Of Loss

There is some compulsion that drives people in our society to try and recoup losses through the same process in which the losses were generated - even if it is illogical to think that such a process is likely to result in recouping the losses. Thus, the gambler who loses in roulette typically tries to recoup his losses in roulette and not by switching to the crap table. Indeed, if the gambler does change games, he or she often considers the loss to be taken and the change is viewed as a new start.

This psychological compulsion has had some very sad effects on investors in the stock market. Some investors - including professional money managers and sophisticated investors - having developed a particular strategy, will continue to employ a losing strategy rather than change to a new strategy.

The investor in options must be careful not to fall into this, or any other, form of compulsive behavior. In market terminology this is called "discipline." The option trader should try and exercise discipline and see things for what they are.

There is a second psychological component which

seems to play a part in the psychology of option writing. As a child I used to bet with my friends on the flip of a coin. If after flipping the coin five times the coin came up heads each of those five times, I was more likely to bet on tails on the sixth flip of the coin. All competent statisticians will tell you that the sixth flip of the coin is not different statistically than each of the prior five flips. That is, there is a 50-50 chance that the coin will come up heads on the sixth flip just as there was on each of the prior flips. Yet, the human mind somehow ascribes a higher likelihood to change than no change.

This false perception also plays a part in the market. Many option writers are trapped into believing that when the market goes up, it must come back down. Many of these beliefs are codified into popular market slogans, such as "what goes up must come down."

Because of the limited life of options, even if the saying is true (and it isn't), it doesn't apply to option writing. As the market goes up, it can continue to go up well beyond the expiration date of the options. It can go up beyond the expiration date of the new options written as the old options begin to lose value. It can go up and up and up, while some make money and some lose money, just as it can go down and down and down.

Therefore, in determining when to modify and option position before expiration, the important consideration should be to maintain the same strategy as originally conceived and to limit and reduce the risk of loss. The general principles to follow in this connection are:

1. When an option position begins to lose money, close it out.

2. In rolling an option position (the meaning of this is discussed below) ask yourself the question: "is this an appropriate initial position to put on, irrespective of what has happened in the past?"

3. Also ask yourself the question: "is this new position consistent with my original strategy?"

The most important single aspect of the psychology of option writing is to recognize that option writing is a statistical process. The option writer tries to capture premiums based on accepting risk. Accepting risk means that there will be some losses and some profits. <u>The option writer must therefore be willing to accept losses and base the expectation of profit on there being more profit positions written than loss positions.</u>

B. Margin and Commission Considerations

After self-reflection, the next most important consideration in modifying an option position may be commissions. Commissions are the nasty topic rarely dealt with in option treatises. The custom seems to be to acknowledge that illustrations exclude transactions costs, including commissions, and to briefly mention the fact that commissions can be a significant factor in option writing.

In fact, commissions can very often be the determining factor in option writing as to whether or not the writer makes a profit or a loss. In writing options between 10 and 50 contracts, the most favorable commission structure that I have ever been able to negotiate is to pay approximately $25 commission for each 10 contracts traded. This is only $0.025 per share. A typical charge for a top non-institutional investor in today's competitive market is $0.04 per share. This comes to $100 per 25 contracts, or $800 in putting on and closing out a 25 contract box spread. I know that some institutional investors pay less than that, and I know that some institutional investors have particular arrangements with brokerage houses where they pay only a commission on opening the option transaction, and nothing on closing it. It is not uncommon, however, for investors to pay as much as $120 commission for each 10 contracts.

An option writer writing a box spread, which consists of four separate options at a time, can therefore be paying almost as much in commissions (if the box spread is opened and all of the position subsequently closed out) as is collected in premiums! This would make it very difficult to earn a profit from writing. For this reason, it is almost mandatory that the serious option writer negotiates a reduced commission structure with the broker.

Commissions become an important factor in option writing in the determination of closing out a profit position. For example, suppose that when the OEX was $320, I wrote 10 CALL spreads, selling the 330's and buying the 340's. Now the market drops precipitously to $280. Both my long and short positions have declined in value, the short position now costing 1/8th of a point and the long position having a value of 1/16th of a point: so the spread could be closed out for a cost of 3/16, or $37.50 plus commissions. With commissions, the net cost of closing out this position will be say, $117.50.

If I do nothing, the options will expire worthless unless the market rebounds past $330. If I close out the position, I will lock in a profit of my net premium less $117.50.

Which decision I make obviously will depend on my judgment at the time, which will, of course, include such factors as the length of time remaining on the options and the commission cost to close out the position. One choice which is commonly made in this situation is to close out the short position, which is the only position at risk, at a cost of $66.25, and leave the long position in place, in the vague hope that the market could strongly rebound and the position either generate a profit or be utilized again as a hedge for writing a new short position of significant premium.

Another decision to make is whether or not to use a discount broker or a full service broker. While some of the discount brokers charge less than full service brokers, I personally prefer the full service broker for regular option trading. The full service broker will call you if a problem is imminent, and will work on getting trades made within a range of discretion, which most discount brokers will not do. And if I'm out of touch for a few days, I feel safer leaving instructions with a broker I know well and speak with frequently. Never the less, I know option traders who use discount brokers without problems and save a great deal of money on commissions. And the best option software available for the moment in on discount broker sites, such as Charles Schwab.

Along with commissions, each brokerage house sets margin requirements, some of which are mandated by federal law and some by stock exchange rules. In considering option writing you should be sure to have adequate capital to cover the "worst case." Many option writers maintain a stock or bond portfolio in the option account to cover margin requirements. Options are then written to hedge against a decline in the bond values (because of an increase in interest rates) and CALLS are written against the stocks. The underlying portfolio thus does double-duty.

C. Recognizing Loss -
Accepting A "Fresh Start"

The most important damage control mechanism in writing options is to close out a position at a predetermined loss. Thus, many out-of-the-money option writers decide in advance (and may even instruct the broker in advance) to close out a spread when the short position is at-the-money. For example:

When the OEX is at $300, I sell the 310 CALLS and buy the 320's. When the OEX moves up to $310, I close out the position at a loss, by buying back the 310 CALLS (at a cost greater than I sold them) and selling the 320's (at a slight profit, perhaps). By closing out the position before the short position becomes in-the-money, I pay out only the increased difference in the time value premium and avoid paying out any intrinsic value premium.

Each investor should make a decision as to how much loss should be accepted when putting on a position. This decision should be determined by such factors as the amount of premium received on the position and the potential risk of allowing the position to get in-the-money. For example, if a $3,000 premium was received for a spread with a maximum potential loss of $5,000, the investor would be more likely to allow the position to get in-the-money than in the case where a relatively small premium, compared to potential loss, has been received.

D. Rolling A Position Up or Down

When the position has been closed out, a common loss mitigation strategy is to roll the position up or down. (See Figure V-1.) At the same time, the position can be rolled "out," which means to a later calendar date, thereby capturing a new, larger premium.

When I close out the position described above (short OEX 310 and long OEX 320), I now write a new CALL spread which is again approximately 10 points out-of-the-money: I sell the 320 CALLS and buy the 325's or 330's. If the new CALL spread has the same expiration date as the old CALL spread, I have rolled up the CALL spread. If I write the new position also for a later calendar date, I have rolled "up and out."

Obviously the same strategy can be employed with PUTS: On May 1 I write a June Put spread when the OEX is at $300; I sell the 290 PUTS and buy the 280 PUTS. By May 15 the OEX has declined to $289. I now close out the original PUT spread and write a new PUT spread by selling the 280's and buying the 270's. I made a profit on the long 280 PUTS, but lost considerably more on the 290 short positions. But the loss was temporarily made up by the premium from the new spread. Unless the market declines below $280 I will not lose any money, but I also will not garner the premium I had hoped to keep from the sale of the first spread.

FIGURE V-1 Rolling Up a CALL Spread That Gets In-the-Money.

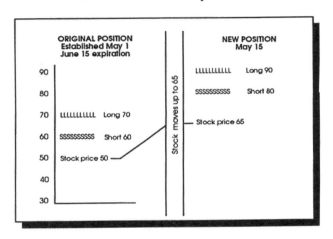

Typical prices – prices at 10 options:

Original position:	Received for $60 short CALLS	$1,000
	Paid for $70 long CALLS	$500
	NET RECEIVED	$500

To close out original position:

	Paid to buy back $60 short CALLS	$7,000
	Received from sale of $70 CALLS	$4,000
	Loss	($3,000)
	Net loss so far	($2,500)

Received on new spread $500

If the new spread is "rolled out" to a calendar date beyond June 15th, $1,000 or more might be received, further mitigating the losses.

In volatile markets, where the need to roll a position is likely, some option writers take more risk at the outset by writing a wider spread, in the anticipation of having to roll it up or down. By leaving more room in the spread, the same long position can be maintained, a greater initial premium received because of the reduced cost of the long position and commissions can be reduced by not having to close out the initial long position.

For example: When the OEX is at $300, I sell the 310 CALLS and buy the 330 CALLS. I get a good premium on the 310's, because it is close to the money and pay very little for the 330's, which are way out-of-the-money. If the market moves up, I can buy back the 310's and write the 315's, 320's, or the 325's. I have room to roll up three different times if it becomes necessary. I can maintain the long 330 position throughout the period as a hedge for whatever short position or positions I decide to take.

Another form of rolling consists of closing out the profitable short position and rewriting it closer to the money. For example: when the OEX is at $300, I write the 310 CALLS, buy the 315 CALLS, write the 290 PUTS and buy the 285 PUTS. I collect a net premium of $2,000 and have a risk of loss of $5,000 less the premium received i.e., $3,000 maximum loss.

Now the OEX moves to $305. The PUT spread declines in value. I can now close out the spread, or - if I so elect - buy back only the short position of the PUT spread, the 290's - and write the 295's. I have rolled up the PUT spread, and taken a profit on the 290's. My new risk is different than my original risk: my original risk was five points in either direction out-of-the-money. My new risk is ten point in the PUT and five points in the CALL, but I now have more premium in hand and less time before expiration.

Rolling the profitable side of a box spread is often coupled with also rolling the loss side. The combination of the new premium on the profit side and the new premium on the loss side can be a strong mitigating factor controlling potential losses or maintaining an initial profit. For example, in the box spread described above, at the same time I roll up the PUT spread to the 295's, I roll up the CALL spread by buying back the 310 CALLS, selling the original 315 CALLS I purchased, selling more 315 CALLS to develop a short position and buying the 320 CALLS. The result is a new CALL spread at 315 short vs. 320 long. In effect I've moved the box parallel with the market. Commissions become a major factor in these determinations.

E. Hedging A Position

Another way to control or mitigate losses is to hedge the position after it has been placed. The hedging can be used either to lock in a profit or to prevent a further loss. There are generally three ways of hedging a position:

1. Buying stock;

2. Buying an option;

3. Selling an option or a spread.

There is a very wide range of examples which could illustrate the use of these techniques in various situation. For illustrative purposes, I am giving one example of each:

Example 1: <u>Buying stock</u>

On April 1, when XXX is at $50, I sell a CALL spread on XXX Co. By selling ten XXX 55 CALLS and buying ten XXX 60 CALLS with an expiration date of May 20. By April 15, XXX stock has gone to 55 and my short position is at-the-money. Not wanting to risk a loss of $1,000 per point on XXX stock, wanting to retain the net premium received on the spread and having confidence that XXX stock will continue to rise, I buy 1,000 shares of XXX stock. Now for every point that XXX stock goes up until $60 I will make $1,000 of unrealized profit on the stock and lose $1,000 on the spread position. If XXX goes back down below $55 during the option period, I will have an unrealized loss on the stock, but not lose anything on the spread and retain the premium received as a hedge against the cost of the stock.

The worst case is if XXX goes to $60 and I lose $5,000 (less the premium) on the option and immediately after the options expire the stock drops to or below my cost. This is called "being whipsawed."

Example 2: Buying an option

To protect an underlying stock portfolio in a market you think will decline, you can buy PUTS. You can buy them on specific stocks, or - if you have a broadly based port-folio, you can buy those index PUTS which most closely follow your stocks.

Many option traders, when buying PUTS to hedge, will simultaneously sell an out-of-the-money CALL. The pre-mium from the CALL offsets some part of the PUT cost and the positions are consistent (bearish).

Example 3: Selling an option to hedge a deteriorating spread

On April 2, with the OEX at $305, I put on an OEX CALL spread by selling the May 310 CALLS and buying the 320's. I collect $300 net premium per option. I do 10 con-tracts at all times.

By May 10 the OEX has moved against me to $315. (See Figure V-2.) Now my financial position is as follows:

1. I collected $3,000 in original premium.

2. The 320 CALLS can be sold for $1,000.

FIGURE V-2 Selling an Option to Hedge a Loss.

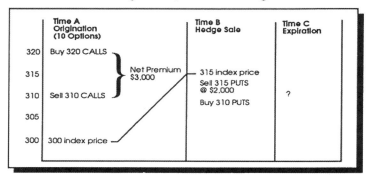

Time A. The potential loss at the origination of the position is $7,000 ($10,000 for the 10 points between 310 and 320 less $3,000 collected in premium. The investor was willing to risk $7,000 for a $3,000 premium because the CALL spread, when put on, was substantially Out-of-the-Money.

Time B. When the index goes to 315, the short position goes "In-the-Money" 5 points, creating a loss of $5,000 in intrinsic value, plus something for Time Value Premium. The amount of Time Value Premium loss should normally be substantially offset by the increase in Time Value Premium of the long position (the 320 CALLS), and, of course, is offset by the new premium.

At this time, the investor sells a PUT spread to hedge. Perhaps a 2 point premium can be received since the short PUT is "At-the-Money" and the market is volatile and bullish. The receipt of $2,000 in premium helps to hedge the potential loss.

Time C. If the market stays at 315 until expiration, the $2,000 premium reduces the loss. If the market goes down, until 310 the investor reduces the loss by $1,000 per point, but suffers a new loss of the same amount on the PUT. If the market continues to rise (which is what is being hedged against) there is the potential for $5,000 of loss, but the total loss risk has been reduced from $7,000 to $5,000.

Two variations are possible, depending on the premium levels and the investor's prediction of the market: (1) The hedge could be a PUT that is "Out-of-the-Money", such as, here, the 310 PUT could be sold, and the 305 bought This produces a smaller premium but allows for less of a "locked-in" loss if the market reverses and goes down. (2) Alternatively, one could sell an "In-the-Money" PUT — here the 320 — and collect an additional $5,000 of intrinsic premium. The sale of the "In-the Money" PUT (the 320) is a powerful way to recap the potential loss if the market continues to rise, but it is not profitable if the market stabilizes at 315.

3. The 310 CALLS will cost me $7,000 to buy back.

4. My net position at this time is therefore negative $3,000.

The potential loss of the original position is $10,000 less the $3,000 premium received or $7,000.

With the index at $315, the short position is "in-the-money" 5 points, creating a loss of $5,000 in intrinsic value.

I then sell a PUT spread hedge, by selling the 315 PUT and buying the 310 PUT. Perhaps a $3,000 premium can be obtained to help hedge the potential loss.

Here are the possible results at expiration:

1. If the OEX goes above $320 I will lose $10,000 on the CALL spread, less the $6,000 in total premium collected, for a net loss of $4,000. The PUT spread saved me $3,000 in a fast rising market in which I otherwise would have had a $7,000 loss.

2. When the OEX is between $315 and $320 I will lose $5,000 at $315 and $10,000 at $320 on the CALL spread less the $6,000 premium received for a net of:

320 - $4,000

319 - $3,000

318 - $2,000

317 - $1,000

316 - $0

315 + $1,000

3. If the OEX is between $310 and $315 I will lose between $0 (at $315) and $5,000 (at $310) on the PUT spread and lose between $5,000 (at $315) and $0 (at $310) on the CALL spread or a net loss of $5,000 on the box. The $6,000 premium received would then result in a net profit of $1,000.

4. When the OEX falls below $310 I will lose $5,000 on the new PUT spread and gain $6,000 in total premium collected for a net of $1,000 profit.

Mitigating strategies can become very complex, but they are an essential part of option writing. The key is to take your time to work them out and to plan them out - to some degree - in advance of the market move. This is not so difficult to do when the hedging is part of the overall strategy from the beginning - such as buying a PUT at the same time as buying stock, or selling stock in a portfolio and buying CALLS to replace it (neither of which strategies I particularly recommend).

What is difficult is to be prepared for contingencies. Have some ideas of what to do in the event of change when you first put on the position.

Part VI - Tax Considerations

The taxation of options is very complex and goes beyond the scope of this book. As a practical matter, almost all of the past tax deferral advantages to options have been eliminated and the option investor should expect to pay income tax at his customary rate on any gains and generally only offset losses over $3,000 against any other capital gains (in the current year or in the future).

Many option writers take losses on year end positions to offset other gains. In doing so, be careful to avoid the wash sale rule. Methods of hedging during such a 30 day period without running afoul of the wash sale rule are complex, as the tax laws, regulations and interpretations so often vary. When problems arise, you should talk to your accountant. But make sure your accountant knows the taxation of options.

One important point to remember arises in writing calls against a portfolio with a low cost basis. Unlike the buy-write situation, if low basis stock is called away it can create a serious and unexpected tax bill, even if the trades were profitable. The investor, broker or advisor must be very sensitive to this issue when writing CALLS against low basis stocks and the broker or advisor should be sure to fully advise the customer of this additional risk and should work with the customer's accountant to reduce any adverse impact from stock being inadvertently called away. A good broker will purchase stock to cover any call so as to avoid the low basis stock from being sold to cover the call.

While it is beyond the scope of this book to cover most of the tax issues that arise with options, there is one that arises often, and therefore is worth mentioning.

When you write a covered call and the stock goes way over the strike price, there is sometimes a potential tax advantage in selling the underlying stock and substituting a long option as a hedge for the remaining short option.

For example: I owned 1000 shares of IBM stock for over one year at a cost of $84. When IBM was at $85 I wrote the 90 calls and took in $2,000. The stock then went to 99. I then sold the stock at 99 and took in a $15,000 profit which will be taxed at the advantageous long term capital gains rate. This left me with a short call at 90, which was $9 in the money (a potential loss of $9,000). To hedge against a continued increase in the stock price, I bought the 100 calls. I could have purchased calls beyond the date of the short position, with the thought that the value would hold up through that date and I would sell before the decline curve (as discussed in prior chapters). In this particular case, however, I purchased long calls that expire on the same date as the short position. I paid $2,000 for the long calls.

So I gave back my option premium. But my worst case is that the stock will rise to over $100 per share and stay there until the termination date. In that case I will make a $15,000 capital gain, and take a $10,000 loss that I can use to offset other premiums that would be taxed at ordinary rates ($3,000 of this loss can even offset ordinary income). Even if the profit and loss were the same, there would be a tax advantage. And there is the possibility that the stock price will now decline, in which case I will have locked in my profit, and my loss will decline.

But as so often is the case, you need to check with your CPA to see if this potential advantage works for you and doesn't run afoul of the very complex tax rules that apply to option transactions.

PART VII - Lessons to be Learned

A. Three Keys to Keeping Brokers Out of Trouble

In the world of option trading the keys for brokers to use to keep out of trouble are:

1. Proper customer selection;

2. Following a consistent strategy.

3. Adequate communication of the strategy, the risk, and the potential dollar loss to the client.

1. Customer Selection

There are at least three questions to ask yourself before you agree to deal in options for a client:

A. Is it the client's money? If the client is acting as a fiduciary for another, for example, as a family trustee, or for a pension plan - different laws and rules apply. As a general matter I would never write even covered CALLS for a fiduciary without clear evidence- - the best is a legal opinion from the customer's lawyer- - that option trading is legally permitted for that trust. I would be very wary of doing option strategies not labeled "conservative strategies" in this book for such a client, irrespective of the trust instrument, with the possible exception of a trustee who is an experienced professional option trader.

B. Can the client bear the loss of the worst case risk? Many clients use the options market as an outlet for gambling instinct. In some ways, this is a socially desirable outlet maybe better than alternatives which offer less chance and may be illegal. Like gambling in general, there can be appropriate situations - a game of gin rummy at the club for a penny a point - and inappropriate ones - taking the family savings to Las Vegas. Allowing clients to risk the family homestead in the option market is no different. Therefore, thoroughly discuss the client's financial position and discretionary capital and don't be afraid to say no to an order that you disagree with or place a trade and then mark the confirm "unsolicited," thinking that this will save you from liability. In the long run the client will have more respect for you and believe in your integrity.

C. Does the client know what he or she is doing? This seems to me to be the weakest area for brokers. Because the truth is, many non-professionals in the options market don't really understand it and are relying on the broker. In these situations, the broker is really taking discretion without acknowledging it and without obtaining the proper forms and approvals.

If your client wants to trade in options and is in a financial position to do so, consider the following;

a. Don't rely on the client reading the prospectuses sent, or the C.B.O.E. pamphlet on options. It's a fact of life that very few clients ever look at this stuff.

b. It is not enough for the client to just say "yes" to each of your suggestions and acknowledge when the trade is complete. If there is a loss the client did not expect, the chances are he or she will sue.

c. I strongly suggest the following: First, bring an unsophisticated customer into the office and have the customer sit with you while you make a few trades. This converts the experience from one of just words to actually doing it.

Second, with appropriate manager approval, send a letter to the customer confirming the option strategies to be followed and delineating the dollar risks. (See Figures VI-1 and VI-2 for examples of such letters.) One advantage to sending the customer a letter confirming a strategy to be followed is that it forces the broker to follow that strategy or the broker may face serious criticism.

Figure VII-1   Sample Letter to Covered Out-of-the-money
CALL Writing Client.

Dear Sam:

*This will confirm our plan to begin writing covered calls against
your portfolio in an attempt to generate additional current income.*

*Since you currently hold 1,000 shares each of IBM, Ford and
GM, we will be writing 10 CALLs of various time periods against
each of these positions. In general we will try to find CALLs with
strike prices that are between 5% and 15% above the current
prices of the stock.*

*As I explained to you, if the stock against which CALLs have
been written goes up to or over the strike price, the stock may
be bought from you at the strike price. You should check with
your tax advisor to see if it is a good (or bad) idea to sell any of
these stocks. The sale can be avoided by either buying back
the options, or covering the CALL by purchasing new stock at
the market price, to deliver to the buyer.*

*Note that when this happens significantly more commissions
result. Also bear in mind that if the stock goes up dramatically,
it can be very expensive to do this.*

*For example, your IBM stock is now $115. We can get two
points for the June 125 CALLs, which will net you approximately
$1,940 after commissions. If IBM stock goes to $159 in the next
60 days (and it has been there before!), it would cost well over
$25,000 to buy back the option, and over $150,000 to buy the
1000 shares of stock needed to meet the call and retain your
original holdings.*

*Please call me if this is in any way not clear, and feel free to
come into the office and watch some trading if you want to learn
more about the option market.*

Sincerely,   Cecilia

Figure VII-2 Sample Letter to Uncovered Writing Client.

Dear Mr. Smythe, Jr.:

This will confirm that we have now begun writing uncovered combinations in your account.

As I understand the strategy you are following, you are writing an out-of-the-money CALL and an out-of-the-money PUT on certain stocks which you follow. Your strategy is to write far enough out-of-the-money to capture the two premiums when the stock volatility maintains the stock price between your parameters, and to hedge or roll when either side gets in-the-money.

As you know, writing these combinations subjects you to very high risk of loss if the market is strongly volatile in either direction. For example, in Oct. 1987, the market dropped over 500 points in a few days, the option market was non-liquid, and PUT option prices soared. Under such circumstances, a short combination such as you recently wrote, with 25 contracts on each side, could lose well over $1 million in a 500 point drop.

While your financial position, as set forth in your Jan. 1988 statement, reflects enough net worth to sustain such a loss, I do want to suggest that you consider buying a hedge position on each side to limit the potential losses from your positions.

Please feel free to call me or come into the office if you wish to explore this in greater depth.

Sincerely,

Ambrose

Finally, do not depend on your compliance staff; check yourself to see that the client has executed the proper option trading forms, that the specific strategies in use are on the forms, and that the financial data is current. If the financial data is not current, send a letter asking for an update.

2. Following A Consistent Strategy

Sometimes brokers act in an inconsistent way out of ignorance. But more often they try to recoup losses, to maintain the customer, by taking greater risk. It is not uncommon to see an out-of-the-money option writer suddenly begin to write deep in the money options to generate cash in an account that has sustained major losses. This change of strategy - eliminating the "window of profit" - is usually not justified and puts the client at greater risk than the original strategy.

Sometimes one sees the converse - a successful, profitable strategy that goes to the broker's head, so the broker becomes more aggressive - for example, the broker may change from writing CALL spreads to writing uncovered CALLS.

The safest way to protect yourself against criticism is to clearly define one or more strategies (i.e., covered CALL writing out-of-the-money, letting stock be called away) and stick to them. Accept losses and reach an agreement on new or changed strategies when appropriate, then confirm the changes by letter.

3. Adequate Communication Of Strategy And Method

How much needs to be communicated and how much confirmed in writing? Not too much. As long as the communication meets three tests:

1. Name the strategy;

2. Leave open the door for more information;

3. State - in dollars - the risk level, where appropriate.

In my opinion, the use of letters of this type would eliminate much of the conflict and litigation that exist in option trading and I do not understand why brokers and brokerage firms do not begin to use them on a regular basis.

B. LESSONS FOR LAWYERS

In large part, the lessons to be learned for lawyers derive from the suggestions made to brokers - were these recommendations followed or not? Unfortunately, the way lawyers traditionally look at stock market cases is often not appropriate. For example, in stock cases one compares the investment with the commissions generated, or one looks at "turnover," the ratio of sales to holdings. These are not very good indices of improper options trading.

In trading options, one expects greater commissions; the box spread above consists of four options for each combination put on. Because of the limited life of options, by definition there is more turnover.

The lawyer handling options controversies and trying to analyze what went wrong is often burdened by having a client. The claimant may exaggerate his or her lack of information about the strategies and the trades. The broker may try to hide the degree of control exercised by the broker over the decision making and often fails to volunteer the real reasons behind certain strategies. For example, out-of-the-money option writers sometimes switch to deep in-the-money writing to generate larger cash balances. And one sometimes sees a steady increase in the number of options bought or sold, as losses are incurred - a familiar form of "doubling up" as it is called in Las Vegas. This may be appropriate if disclosed to the client, but is sometimes used to cover-up losses. There may be an inappropriate change to a higher risk strategy.

And it pays to be paranoid: the first option case I handled as a lawyer was confusing to me at first, because I couldn't understand the customer's motives (my client) for some of the things he did with respect to the broker. It was only after a two week trial in federal court that I learned that the customer and the broker were in a sexual relationship together, and the business my client gave to the broker was really payment for sexual favors.

The approach I recommend for lawyers is to identify the strategy or strategies employed and to determine the answers to the following questions:

a. Were they consistently followed?

b. Were they appropriate for this client?

c. Were they communicated to the client?

d. Did the client understand?

e. Even if the strategies were communicated, was the degree of risk and the potential dollar loss communicated and understood?

f. Did the client correctly disclose to the broker the client's true financial position and willingness and ability to accept losses?

g. What level of participation did the client have in the extent and level of trading and the acceptance of risk?

In many cases, pursuing the answers to these questions leads one to the conclusion that some blame for the losses falls on both sides to the controversy. Thus, it is not uncommon for courts, juries and arbitrators to reach compromise decisions. Often both sides are unhappy with such decisions because both sides come out with financial losses in such cases, particularly after payment of attorneys' fees. It is, therefore, important for the lawyer handling such cases to communicate to the client those facts which the lawyer discovers which point to fault by the lawyer's client, so that the client does not have unrealistic expectations.

A recurring theme in options controversies boils down to a question of timing. Learning is a process and clients often learn about options during the process of watching the trades suggested by the broker. When a loss occurs in the middle of such a process, the question that arises is where the client was in the learning process.

In one famous court case, the court was faced with such a situation. The essence of the court's holding was that the customer was inexperienced during the first year of trading and thus the broker was responsible for losses during that period. But after a year of trading the customer was sufficiently knowledgeable to evaluate the risk himself. Thus, losses in year two were not recoverable.

I once handled a case with a variation on this theme. The client put himself in the hands of a broker who made inappropriate trades, some of which were made while the client was out of the country. When the client returned and discovered extensive losses and trades, he angrily accused the broker of fraud and deception. The broker admitted his errors and begged for another chance to make up the losses. The client agreed, thinking that the broker was so afraid of disclosure that he would see that profits were generated. Further losses resulted. The arbitrators in this matter awarded reimbursement of the losses before discovery, but not those arising afterward. This seems consistent with the court's decision in the case above.

C. Using Professional Witnesses

A group of expert witnesses has evolved who testify in option cases. Naturally, these witnesses, the lawyers from the firms handling the bulk of the cases - (usually the defense side), and the arbitrators all know each other. Needless to say, this doesn't hurt the defense of these cases, since the same lawyers appear regularly on the defense, but the plaintiff lawyer group is much more diverse.

In complex cases, these experts can be extremely helpful - perhaps indispensable. Even with such experts available, a lawyer knowledgeable about options is a major asset in options cases, because the expert testimony involving judgment is often skewed and biased.

For example: Beware of exaggeration by the claimant's expert. In writing a naked CALL, the risk is theoretically infinite. The expert can, therefore, claim that hundreds of thousands of dollars were at risk, which is a larger risk than the net worth of the claimant should bear. While the conclusion may be correct, the dollar figure is often exaggerated. The upside of a particular stock in a 30-day period can be historically and statistically evaluated and is not really infinite.

By the same token, if IBM stock is at $100, and a 100 PUT is written, while the theoretical loss is 100 points, as a practical matter it is virtually impossible for IBM stock to go to zero. Even companies that go into bankruptcy normally retain some stock value. Furthermore, remember that the brokerage house will typically sell out a customer when the loss reaches a certain point, if the customer has not covered the new margin requirement. So this is typically the point at which the maximum loss can be quantified. For example, a customer with $10,000 in equity might be sold out if the stock dropped form $100 to $90 and therefore really only has a downside risk potential of $10,000, not $100,000.

On the defense side, this fact can be taken advantage of by explaining that while there was no downside hedge position written, as a practical matter there is a stop loss near the margin requirement, so the customer is protected to that extent. This is generally true, although in a few cases the market has dropped too fast for the broker to sell out the client at the desired level.

One should also be aware of expert testimony which is theoretically correct, but not of substantive value to the case in point.

For example, naked writing on the OEX is arguably less risky than naked writing on specific stocks. This is because in writing, say, a PUT against a stock like IBM, there is always the possibility of unusual and specific news about IBM causing a sudden and unexpected decline in the stock. This can be news as innocuous as reduced earnings, or as serious as the massive fraud that was discovered at Enron. But, in writing against the OEX, these "blips" are substantially reduced. Even if sudden unexpected information is discovered about one company that makes up a part of the index, it will not have that much of an effect on the overall index. There is, therefore, less risk in writing on the OEX than in writing against specific stocks. From this point of view, it can be honestly said that writing naked options on the OEX has a certain conservative nature to it, but this is more of a theoretical difference than one of substance.

Because options controversies arise out of an agreement between the customer and the brokerage house, that agreement should be the starting point for the lawyer. Jurisdictions differ in a number of legal rules involving these controversies, but in general, customer agreements usually provide that option controversies (not involving commodities) are subject to mandatory arbitration before either the NASD (National Association of Securities Dealers) or the NYSE (New York Stock Exchange), at the client's election. Each of these bodies publishes books explaining their procedures, and setting forth their rules, which should be carefully reviewed.

PART VIII - Conclusion

Options can be an interesting and profitable investment. They can provide a source of income. They can also be used to protect other investments. Because of their limited life and the complexity of many option strategies, option trading requires more knowledge and more attention than other stock market investments. Option writing is not for dilettantes, or for those who cannot psychologically accept losses from time-to-time.

Many option investors lose money in unexpected amounts because they fail to understand the basic difference between buying something and selling first with a potential obligation to buy back later. They fail to assimilate the potential for ending up with a debit balance, requiring the payment of more funds than originally required (unlike the purchase situation).

Option BUYERS usually lose money. By the nature of the market and premium prices only the clairvoyants seem to profit from the pure purchase of an option.

The use of high risk, or open-ended loss potential

strategies is only appropriate for a limited number of investors and should be avoided except where many factors are confirmed and well communicated.

The use of inconsistent strategies, strategies inappropriate to the investor, or strategies not fully understood by both the investor and the broker should be avoided. In the case of controversies, inconsistent and inappropriate strategies can result in liability to the broker.

In spite of the many who lose, there are a number of conservative option strategies, not well known to non-professional investors, that offer a statistically reasonable likelihood of profit within the confines of defined dollar risk.

The use of the strategies described here, or the use of options to protect other investments, offers a conservative, appropriate investment vehicle for most investors.